The ABCs of ACOs

A PRACTICAL HANDBOOK ON ACCOUNTABLE CARE ORGANIZATIONS

Raymund C. King, MD, JD
Rachel V. Rose, JD, MBA
Martin R. Merritt, JD
John Okray, JD, MBA, LLM

American Bar Association Health Law Section
Tort Trial & Insurance Practice Section

Cover design by Amanda Fry/ABA Publishing.

Printed in the United States of America.

18 17 16 15 14 5 4 3 2 1

Library of Congress Cataloging-in-Publication Data

The ABCs of ACOs : a practical handbook on accountable care organizations / By Rachel V. Rose, Raymund C. King, Martin R. Merritt, John Okray.
p. cm.
Includes bibliographical references and index.
ISBN 978-1-62722-626-4 (alk. paper)
1. Accountable care organizations (Medical care)--Law and legislation--United States. 2. Health facilities--Law and legislation--United States. 3. Medical care--Law and legislation--United States. 4. Medical laws and legislation--United States. I. Rose, Rachel V. author.
KF3825.A91 2014
344.7303'21--dc23

2014025801

Contents

Introduction and Ground Rules: The ABCs of Physician-Owned ACOs

Imagine yourself watching a car that is speeding down the road toward a brick wall. The brick wall represents the year 2020, when the United States will begin experiencing a significant increase—some report as much as an 80 percent increase—in health care demands in this country just from the "baby boomer effect."

Imagine that Daddy is driving the car, and Mommy is arguing with Daddy. Mommy and Daddy represent Congress and our government. Mommy and Daddy are arguing so vigorously against each other that neither one is really paying much attention to the fast-approaching brick wall, and both are only focused upon jockeying for position in their arguments regarding the car—hoping that the passengers in the back seat will take notice of who is winning the debate.

Now, imagine that you (the consumer, the registered voter, the health care provider, etc.) are sitting in the back seat of this car, and you find an oddly shaped seat belt that you cannot quite figure out how to use. You just know the basics on how to brace yourself for an impact, and you are doing everything you can to get into position so that when the car actually hits the wall you are not seriously injured.

The Patient Protection and Affordable Care Act, commonly called the Affordable Care Act (ACA) or "Obamacare" by some, is a United States federal statute that was signed into law by President Barack Obama on March 23, 2010. Together with the Health Care and Education Reconciliation Act (HCERA), it is perhaps the most significant regulatory overhaul of the United States health care system since the creation of Medicare and Medicaid in 1965.

On paper, the goals of the ACA are to increase the quality and affordability of health insurance, lower the uninsured rate by expanding public and private insurance coverage, and reduce the costs of health care for individuals and the government. It provides a number of mechanisms, which include mandates, subsidies, and insurance exchanges, to increase coverage and affordability. The ACA also requires insurance companies to cover all applicants within new minimum standards and offer the same rates regardless of pre-existing conditions or gender. The Congressional Budget Office (CBO) initially projected that the ACA will lower both future deficits and Medicare spending.

On June 28, 2012, the United States Supreme Court upheld the constitutionality of the ACA's individual mandate in *National Federation of Independent Business v. Sebelius*. However, the Court held that states cannot be forced to participate in the ACA's Medicaid expansion under penalty of losing their current Medicaid funding. Since that ruling, the law and its implementation have continued to face challenges in Congress, in federal courts, and from some state governments. Many efforts to oppose, undermine, and repeal the legislation have drawn support from prominent conservative advocacy groups, Congressional and many state Republicans, certain small business organizations, and the Tea Party movement.

The ACA also makes provision for Accountable Care Organizations (ACOs). An ACO is a health care organization composed of health care providers who agree to take on a shared responsibility for the care of a defined population of patients while assuring active management of both the quality and cost of that care. For those ACOs that participate in the Medicare Shared Savings Program (SSP), the ACO must care for at least five thousand (5,000) Medicare-covered lives. An ACO is characterized by a payment and care delivery model that seeks to tie provider reimbursements to quality metrics and reductions in the total cost of care for an assigned population of patients.

The current health care milieu suggests a move away from pure fee-for-service (FFS) arrangements toward a formula that promotes value for patients and efficiency for the system overall. The pay-for-performance (PFP) model requires that providers monitor and manage quality as well as efficiency of health care delivery. In the ACO structure, a good guideline for formation can be found in the model of a Patient Centered Medical Home (PCMH), which utilizes patient registries, team care, care coordination, and health information technology (HIT). These elements of the PCMH will be rewarded with enhanced payments and incentives.

The ACO may use a range of payment models (capitation, fee-for-service with asymmetric or symmetric shared savings, etc.). The ACO is accountable to the patients and the third-party payer for the quality, appropriateness, and efficiency of the health care provided. According to the Centers for Medicare and Medicaid Services (CMS), an ACO is "an organization of health care providers that agrees to be accountable for the quality, cost, and overall care of Medicare beneficiaries who are enrolled in the traditional fee-for-service program who are assigned to it."[1]

The intent of the SSP is to promote accountability for a population of Medicare beneficiaries, improve the coordination of FFS items and services, encourage investment in infrastructure and redesigned care processes for high quality and efficient service delivery, and incentivize higher value care. In order to provide an incentive to ACOs that successfully meet quality and savings requirements, the Medicare Program can share a percentage of the achieved savings with the ACO. Under the SSP, ACOs will only share in savings if they meet both the quality performance standards and generate shareable savings.

The basic ground rules are as follows: The physicians and/or physician groups enrolled in the ACO are identified by their tax ID numbers in order to verify that the ACO provides health care to at least 5,000 Medicare-covered lives—the patients make the preponderance of their outpatient visits to specific health care providers within the ACO. Specialists may join as many ACOs as they wish, but primary care providers may only join one ACO. The physician participants in an ACO each sign a three-year ACO Participant Agreement with CMS.

CMS has established certain "benchmarks" of monetary expenditures for each Medicare region, and it forms the "baseline" of expenditure per patient per year. For example, if the benchmark for a given region is $10,000 per patient per year, then an ACO with 5,000 covered lives represents a total potential of $50,000,000 of health care expenditure.

Theoretically, if the ACO spends less than $10,000 per patient per year, then the difference between that net amount and the benchmark represents the "shared savings" for that ACO. The shared savings are then split equally with CMS at the end of the year. Therefore, if this ACO with 5,000 covered lives spends, let's say, $1,000 less per patient per year, that represents $5,000,000 of health care shared savings per year. That amount of savings is then shared 50/50 with CMS, and $2,500,000 would go to CMS, and the other $2,500,000 would go to the ACO.

But what happens when the ACO spends more than $10,000 per patient per year? In our same example, if the ACO spends $1,000 more per patient per year, that represents $5,000,000 of health care loss—of which $2,500,000 is owed to CMS. Under the current regulations, the ACO may choose only to participate in the upside during the first three years of participation, wherein shared savings are split with CMS.

However, if after three years it appears that there is a loss, the ACO may decide then whether it wants to owe CMS or dissolve as an entity altogether. Indeed, the manner in which the shared savings is calculated and distributed to the partners/members of the ACO should be articulated adequately in the contractual agreements between the parties. Important to note is the fact that if shared savings are the only source of funding for incentives or infrastructure support, there is a danger that the amount of money for those purposes will diminish over time.

CMS has promulgated both a one-sided model (sharing savings, but not losses, for the entire term of the first agreement) and a two-sided model (sharing both savings and losses for the entire term of the agreement), allowing the ACO to opt for either model for their first agreement period. CMS believes this approach will have the advantage of providing an entry point for organizations with less experience with risk models, such as some physician-driven organizations or smaller ACOs, to gain experience with population management before transitioning to a shared-losses model, while also providing an opportunity for more experienced ACOs that are ready to share in losses to enter a sharing arrangement that provides a greater share of savings, but with the responsibility of repaying Medicare a portion of any losses.

Under both models, if an ACO meets quality standards and achieves savings and also meets or exceeds a Minimum Savings Rate (MSR), the ACO will share in savings, based on the quality score of the ACO. ACOs will share in all savings, not just the amount of savings that exceeds the MSR, up to a performance payment limit. Similarly, ACOs with expenditures meeting or exceeding the Minimum Loss Rate (MLR) will share in all losses, up to a loss-sharing limit.

To provide a greater incentive for ACOs to adopt the two-sided approach, the maximum sharing percentage based on quality performance is higher for the two-sided model. ACOs adopting this model will be eligible for a sharing rate of up to 60 percent, while ACOs in the one-sided model will be eligible for a sharing rate of up to 50 percent. Under both models, CMS will base the actual savings percentage for the individual ACO (up to the maximum for that model) on its performance score for the quality measures. As with shared savings, the amount of shared losses will be based in part on the ACO's quality performance score.

Before an ACO can share in any savings created, it must demonstrate that it met the quality performance standard for that year. The four key areas that CMS will focus on for quality measures are:

1. Patient/caregiver experience (seven measures)
2. Care coordination/patient safety (six measures)
3. Preventive health (eight measures)
4. At-risk populations:
    a. diabetes (one measure and one composite consisting of five measures)
    b. hypertension (one measure)
    c. ischemic vascular disease (two measures)
    d. heart failure (one measure)
    e. coronary artery disease (one composite consisting of two measures)

An ACO may be owned by a health care or similar entity, or it may be a physician-owned entity. If it is a physician-owned ACO, at least 75 percent of the ACO must be owned or controlled by the physician provider participants in that ACO.[2] To date, this author has created four ACOs in the state of Texas. The collective wisdom gleaned from the talented subject-matter contributors to this book have been combined with the author's ACO experience, interactions with various ACO groups in the United States, 10 years of experience as a practicing physician, and almost 15 years of experience as a health care lawyer to culminate in this book.

Many seem to be in a quandary about the impact of the ACA and ACOs upon health care delivery in this country. Many have tried to predict the fate of the new health care regulations and the impact upon society and health care. No matter what the conclusion, one thing is sure: The collision with the "baby boomer wall" is inevitable, and we will all feel the impact.

I would like to thank the American Bar Association for the opportunity to publish this book. I would also like to thank Martin Merritt, John Okray, and Rachel Rose for their legal expertise and contributions. This book is intended for lawyers as well as health care providers that are involved in the formation, the maintenance, or the deconstruction of a physician-owned ACO. Our goal is to educate the reader with some real-life applications involving physician-owned ACOs. We foresee that health care is like a vehicle on a collision course with an amorphous wall of increased health care demands from the baby boomers, but armed with the proper education, our hope is that no one goes through the windshield following this "collision."

Raymund C. King, MD, JD
The Law Offices of Raymund C. King, MD, JD, PLLC

Notes

1. Premier Patient Healthcare, http://www.premierphc.com/acomodel.aspx (last accessed May 20, 2014).

2. 76 Fed. Reg. at 67,820.

About the Authors

Dr. Raymund King is the principal and founder of the Law Offices of Raymund C. King, MD, JD, PLLC, in Plano, Texas.

He received his undergraduate degree with honors from the University of Dallas, his medical degree from the University of Texas Medical School in Houston, Texas, and his residency training in Otolaryngology/Head and Neck Surgery at the University of Oklahoma Health Sciences Center prior to going into private practice. Dr. King also had the distinction of being one of the physicians who treated victims of the Oklahoma City bombing at ground zero in 1995.

After ten years of medical practice as an otolaryngologist/head and neck surgeon, Dr. King obtained his law degree from the Oklahoma City University School of Law, and in 2004 he was awarded the Distinguished Young Alumnus Award from the OCU law school.

Dr. King's law firm represents medical and dental groups, accountable care organizations, ambulatory surgery centers, and other health care entities and corporations. He also represents various non-health care corporations in business/corporate matters such as complex mergers and acquisitions. He has multiple publications in the medical and legal arenas, and he combines his experience as a physician with his expertise as a health care and transactional business lawyer to benefit his clients. He is currently on the Book Publishing Board of the American Bar Association, Tort Trial and Insurance Practice Section, and he is general counsel to the Texas Ambulatory Surgery Center Society.

Martin Merritt of Dallas is a 25-year health lawyer with Friedman & Feiger, representing physicians, dentists, nurses, chiropractors, hospitals, ASCs, IPAs, ACOs, group practices, DME suppliers, device manufacturers, drug manufacturers, compounding pharmacies, pharmaceutical companies, investors, management companies, medical testing laboratories, and medical building owners in health care compliance, administrative law, BCBSTX insurance audits, and defense before licensing boards, and in medical ethics, including Stark Law, the AKS, the False Claims Act, CMPL, FDCA misbranding cases, and Texas DTPA actions by the Texas lawyer general, as well as state and federal medical litigation.

Mr. Merritt is a member of the Health Law Section of the Texas Bar Association and the Health Law Section of the Dallas Bar Association. Martin is available to address small or large groups in need of help understanding state and federal health law regulatory compliance.

John Okray is Deputy General Counsel at American Beacon Advisors, Inc., in Fort Worth, Texas. He is the Vice Chair of the Federal Bar Association's Health Law Section, serves on the editorial board of *The Federal Lawyer* magazine, has served in various positions of responsibility within the American Bar Association, and is a Sustaining Life Fellow of the American Bar Foundation. Mr. Okray has represented physicians in matters before state medical boards, peer review organizations, and insurance carrier provider credentialing committees to maintain or restore physician licenses, credentials, and insurance provider participation. He has frequently written on issues of interest to corporate counsel and business lawyers.

Mr. Okray received his BA from the University of Massachusetts Boston, JD from Suffolk University Law School, MBA from Suffolk University Sawyer Business School, and LLM in taxation from Boston University School of Law. He holds the Certified Regulatory and Compliance Professional and Certified Governance, Risk, and Compliance Professional designations from the FINRA Institute at Wharton and Open Compliance and Ethics Group, respectively.

Rachel V. Rose, JD, MBA is a Principal with Rachel V. Rose – Attorney at Law, P.L.L.C. located in Houston, TX.

Ms. Rose has a unique background, having worked in many different facets of healthcare throughout her career including: work in acute care hospitals including the operating room and dietary department; consultative work as a top performing representative for the pharmaceutical and medical device industry; work for the Chairman of the Reform and Oversight Committee on Capitol Hill; intern at the Department of Health and Human Services; and compiling policy papers at the Royal College of Nursing in

London. She has worked on Wall Street and at one of the Big Four consulting firms. Prior to opening her law firm, she was Director of Business Development and Assistant General Counsel for a healthcare advisory company. She is published and presents on a variety of healthcare topics including: the False Claims Act, the Foreign Corrupt Practices Act, physician reimbursement, ICD-10, access to care, anti-kickback and Stark laws, U.S. Supreme Court cases impacting the medical device industry, international comparative healthcare laws, and HIPAA/the HITECH Act.

1

Accountable Care Organizations

A History of the American Health Care System: From "Cash Only" to "Shared Savings" Programs

On March 23, 2010, the Patient Protection and Affordable Care Act, Pub. L. 111-148, was enacted, followed on March 30, 2010, by enactment of the Health Care and Education Reconciliation Act of 2010, Pub. L. 111-152, which amended certain provisions of the Patient Protection and Affordable Care Act (ACA).[1] Collectively known as the "Affordable Care Act," these enactments include a number of provisions designed to improve the quality of Medicare services, support innovation and the establishment of new payment models, better align Medicare payments with provider costs, strengthen program integrity within Medicare, and put Medicare on a firmer financial footing. Regulations for the Shared Savings Program are found at 42 C.F.R. § 425.10 *et seq.*

The Affordable Care Act's Shared Savings Program (SSP) augments, but does not replace, the current Fee-for-Service (FFS) payment model. The regulations under 42 C.F.R. § 425.10 "must not be construed to affect the payment, coverage, program integrity, and other requirements that apply to providers and suppliers under FFS Medicare." Providers continue to be reimbursed based upon evaluation, diagnosis, and treatment, after the patient's condition and treatment plan is reduced to a CPT or ICD-9 Code. Providers converts Diagnosis and treatement to a code. They are paid based on codes. While the FFS coding system accurately matches reimbursement to the diagnosis and treatment provided, the system does not take into account quality, "outcomes," or other "value-based" metrics. Certainly, there is no built-in financial incentive for efforts directed toward maintaining a patient's health in the first place, nor for reimbursing a provider's efforts to ensure the patient is taking responsibility for his or her own condition. Thus, the idea is that we could be doing more with the available dollars if CMS were to provide incentives directed at "quality," "value," and "patient outcomes."

ACOs create incentives for health care providers to work together to treat an individual patient across care settings—including doctor's offices, hospitals, and long-term care facilities. The Medicare Shared Savings Program (SSP) will reward ACOs that lower their growth in health care costs while meeting performance standards on quality of care and putting patients first.[2] There are currently 33 required quality measures that are part of the quality performance standard—including the Consumer Assessment of Healthcare Providers and Systems (CAHPS) patient experience survey measures, claims-based measures, the Electronic Health Record (EHR) Incentive Program measure, and the required Group Practice Reporting Option (GPRO) web interface quality measures—that are required for purposes of ACO participants earning a Physician Quality Reporting System (PQRS) incentive under the Medicare Shared Savings Program.[3]

Many provisions within the Affordable Care Act (ACA) implement value-based purchasing programs. Section 3022 requires the Secretary to establish the Shared Savings Program, intended to encourage the development of Accountable Care Organizations (ACOs) in Medicare. The Shared Savings Program is a key component of the Medicare delivery system reform initiatives included in the Affordable Care Act and is a new approach to the delivery of health care aimed at (1) better care for individuals; (2) better health for populations; and (3) lower growth in Medicare Parts A and B expenditures. This is referred to throughout the Act and regulations as the "Three Part Aim."

Value-based purchasing is a concept that links payment directly to the quality of care provided and is a strategy that can help transform the current payment system by rewarding providers for delivering high-quality, efficient clinical care. CMS views value-based purchasing as an important step to revamping how care and services are paid for, moving increasingly toward rewarding better value, outcomes, and innovations instead of merely increased volume. For a complete discussion, including CMS's goals in implementing value-based purchasing initiatives, please refer to section I.A. of the proposed rule at 76 Fed. Reg. 19530.

In the notice and comment period leading up to the final rule,[4] many participants expressed concern that CMS might invade the province of "Physician Sovereignty" discussed in Paul Starr's seminal work, *The Social Transformation of American Medicine, The Rise of a Sovereign Profession and the Making of a Vast Industry*. In response, CMS makes clear that wherever possible the government has tried to reduce or eliminate prescriptive or burdensome requirements that could discourage participation in the Shared Savings Program. CMS has also been vigilant in protecting the rights and benefits of FFS beneficiaries under traditional Medicare to maintain the same access to care and freedom of choice that existed prior to the implementation of this program. These provisions can be found throughout the final rule.

Health Insurance in America: A Brief History

Germany has the world's oldest national social health insurance system with origins dating back to Otto von Bismarck's social legislation, which included the Health Insurance Bill of 1883.[5] As mandatory health insurance, it originally applied only to low-income workers and certain government employees but gradually expanded to cover the great majority of the German population.

By contrast, in the United States, there was no widely available health insurance coverage until about the early 1930s. If a person required medical care, he or she paid for the service out of pocket. This was a true "supply and demand" system, as the decision to authorize treatment was never divorced from an awareness of the cost. Fee-for-service, and the "usual and customary" rate for such fees, depended entirely upon the patient's ability to pay, and at least to some extent, free-market principles kept costs in check.

The concept of "health insurance" was thought unworkable because of two factors: (1) "moral hazard," meaning the presence of insurance actually encouraged utilization—a condition normally fatal to managing risk; and (2) "adverse selection," meaning only those in need of care (or expecting such need) would buy insurance, then drop coverage once the need passed. Underwriters feared such a system would be populated entirely by the least healthy Americans.

Hospital insurance would not be widely offered in America until the early 1930s when Baylor Hospital in Dallas offered a plan in which a group of teachers paid a small sum to insure a certain number of days of hospital care. This had more to do with "vacancy" than underwriting risk. After Joseph Lister pioneered antiseptic surgical practices, demand for, and the supply of, American hospitals increased exponentially in the run-up to the Great Depression. When the economy faltered, hospitals simply needed a means of attracting patients, and health insurance was reimagined. Even if only the unwell sought coverage, utilization was naturally controlled by limiting the number of days of coverage.

Employer-provided coverage was largely a product of World War II and insured a different kind of market, which was also deceptively inexpensive to cover. A wartime shortage of men and women in the workforce threatened to lead to "wage inflation," at a time when the economy was almost completely devoted to the war effort. In order to hold down costs, the government imposed wage freezes, while exempting a certain percentage of fringe benefits, including employer-provided health insurance. Utilization was controlled because employer-provided plans insured a population of only the healthiest able-bodied workers. Built into this scheme was the near total elimination of "adverse selection." Where it existed, "adverse selection" often favored employers, as workers with family members in need of care were more likely to remain at a job that provided medical coverage.

Medicare and Medicaid Insurance

In 1965, it seemed employer-provided coverage was working perfectly. Every person who wanted a job could find one, all but the most unskilled jobs provided insurance, and most workers did not require a great deal of medical care. It did not seem too difficult to think this success could be transferred to a plan of social insurance. As a social insurance program, however, Medicare and Medicaid spread the financial risk associated with illness across society to protect everyone, and thus had a somewhat different social role from for-profit private insurers, which manage their risk portfolio by adjusting their pricing according to perceived risk.[6] The problem with providing coverage to the elderly and disabled lies in the fact that this is the segment of the population that requires the most care. Nevertheless, after several failed attempts, Congress in 1965 finally passed the Medicare and Medicaid amendments to the Social Security Act, titled, appropriately enough, "Health Insurance for the Aged and Disabled," 42 U.S.C. § 1395, *et seq*.

Conservatives, namely the American Medical Association (AMA), opposed the plan largely because of fear that government money would lead to government takeover and loss of physician autonomy. Desperate to pass the legislation, backers in Congress addressed the problem by (1) promising payment on an FFS basis of the usual and customary charges incurred by the patient, without seeking volume discounts, a promise repeated in 2003 to secure passage of the prescription drug benefit under Medicare Part D, and (2) promising "federal noninterference," which is codified in the first section of the Social Security Act, 42 U.S.C. § 1395.

Forty-five years later, in 2010, Medicare provided health insurance to 48 million Americans—40 million people age 65 and older and eight million younger people with disabilities. Medicare serves a large population of old and disabled individuals. On average, Medicare covers about half (48 percent) of health care costs for enrollees. Medicare enrollees must cover the rest of the cost. These out-of-pocket costs vary depending on the amount of health care a Medicare enrollee needs. They might include uncovered services—such as long-term care, dental, hearing, and vision care—and supplemental insurance.

Medicaid is a means-tested social insurance program funded jointly by the federal and state governments but administered by the states.[7] The Affordable Care Act will significantly expand both eligibility for and federal funding of Medicaid beginning on January 1, 2014. Under the law as written, all U.S. citizens and legal residents with income up to 133 percent of the poverty line, including adults without dependent children, would qualify for Medicaid coverage. Additional federal funding payments to the states under ACA only apply to "newly eligible" Medicaid beneficiaries, not everyone. The United States Supreme Court ruled, in *National Federation of Independent Business v. Sebelius*,[8] that states do not have to agree to this expansion in order to continue to receive existing levels of Medicaid funding, and many states have chosen to continue with current funding levels and eligibility standards.

Beginning in the 1990s, many states received waivers from the federal government to create Medicaid managed care (HMO) programs. Under managed care, Medicaid recipients are enrolled in a private health plan, which receives a fixed monthly premium from the state. The health plan is then responsible for providing all or most of the recipient's health care needs. Today, all but a few states use managed care (HMOs) to provide coverage to a significant proportion of Medicaid enrollees. Nationwide, roughly 60 percent of enrollees are enrolled in managed care (HMO) plans. Core eligibility groups of poor children and parents are most likely to be enrolled in managed care, while the aged and disabled eligibility groups more often remain in traditional "fee for service" Medicare.

Further, ACA calls for the creation of Health Insurance Marketplaces, which are intended to be private insurance policies that are subsidized in whole or in part by federal funds. Thus, ACA greatly expands federal influence into the market of previously uninsured individuals and may bring the host of Federal Fraud, Waste, and Abuse regulation to plans that are subsidized by federal dollars.

It is common for dramatic changes in insurance practices, such as the creation of SSFs, first to occur in publicly administered social insurance programs. If the changes in public plans prove successful, private plans (with no government funding) will normally follow suit. Certainly, the CMS plan for the creation of ACOs will create an investment and delivery infrastructure that can be adapted to private plans.

The primary financial reason for the ACO Shared Savings Program lies in the fact that government forecasters miscalculated the actual cost and too optimistically hoped that Medicare and Medicaid costs would be contained by free-market principles. Government money would attract more providers,

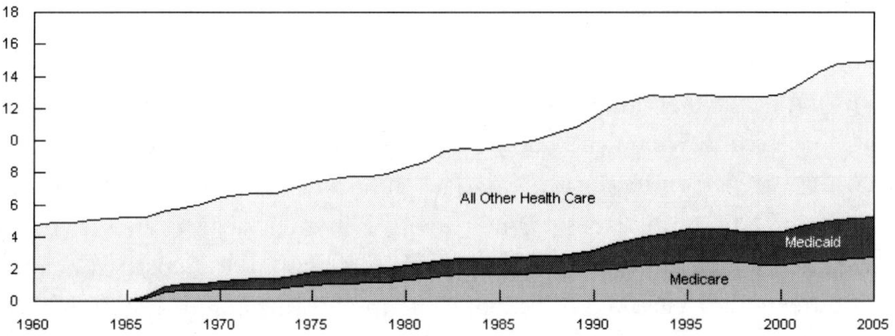

Figure 1.1
Health Care Spending as a Percentage of GDP from 1960–2005

Source: Congressional Budget Office

which should lead to competition based upon price. But free-market principles only apply where the patient is motivated to seek the lowest price. Experience proved the opposite to be true. Patients were attracted to facilities with the latest and most expensive equipment and the most pleasing atmosphere. The elimination of many Certificate of Need laws (which are aimed at restraining health care facility costs and allowing coordinated planning of new services and construction) was intended to lower costs by increasing the number of hospital beds and facilities available to a finite number of patients. Instead, a pattern emerged in which utilization increased with the number of available beds, clinics, and providers. Divorced from concern over price, patients simply did what doctors suggested and chose the most appealing facility available.

Then too, America's postwar dominance as the world's only industrial power could not last forever. As the world rebuilt, jobs and tax money left for foreign shores. This had the dual effect of reducing gross domestic product (and tax revenues) while health care spending continued to climb.

One logical solution might be to attack the problem head on: increase the tax rate and cut benefits. This solution, however, is hugely unpopular with voters.

"A Broke and Broken System"

If cutting benefits and raising taxes is thought to be impossible, we are left with a system in which the public, insurance companies, and health care providers are left to fend for themselves in a state of Fee-for-Service chaos, one in which no one escapes partial responsibility. The health care system in the United States has been described as the world's largest, costliest health care bureaucracy, engulfed by red tape and maddening complexity, in which "[i]nsurers cheat patients and doctors; patients cheat doctors and insurers; doctors cheat insurers and patients; and all cheat the federal government."[9]

Inflating costs have forced many employers to drop coverage, depriving many of health care benefits that cannot be obtained elsewhere. Because the Employee Retirement Income Security Act (ERISA) protects employer-provided plans from liability under state laws aimed at protecting patients from deceptive or unfair insurance practices, employers benefited from such protection, and many plan administrators took full advantage. Post-claims denial of coverage, particularly after the service has been provided, adds to the number of uninsured, straining the finances of hospitals, which are required by the Emergency Medical Treatment & Labor Act (EMTALA) to accept any patient who presents to the emergency room, regardless of ability to pay. Insurance carriers of all stripes began to control costs by engaging in "post-claims underwriting," a process in which the insurer waits until benefits are required, then scours the insurance application, looking for a means to rescind the policy on the basis of an undisclosed condition on the application. Tort reform laws, aimed at lowering the cost of doing business, further add to the woes of hospitals and other providers by limiting casualty insurance payments on account of torts, such as negligence. Tort reform notwithstanding, catastrophically injured patients continue to require care, and that cost must be absorbed by the larger system.

Patients bear responsibility, particularly those who could afford coverage but do not purchase it. If a need arises, many patients consider the emergency room the "family doctor" and have no intention of paying the bill presented. This led to "cost shifting" on the part of hospitals, a practice in which the actual cost of providing care to a patient is dramatically inflated, in hopes of collecting some of the costs associated with treating those who cannot pay.

For its part, the government in the early 1990s, set a course toward increased enforcement of Fraud, Waste, and Abuse laws, such as Stark Law and the Anti-Kickback Statute (AKS), which is terrifying to a largely honest health care industry. While no one is in favor of actual fraud, in order to avoid potential federal liability, physician advocacy groups such as the Association of American Physicians and Surgeons (AAPS) call for physicians to "opt-out"[10] on the grounds that accepting federal and state money is not worth the risk of enforcement activity. Even a technical violation, they argue, regardless of the fact that the patient might need the care provided, could lead to severe penalties and exclusion from the program.[11] The Recovery Audit Contractor (RAC) Audit program is often criticized as a bounty system in which RAC contractors are paid to find even the smallest defect in documentation and coding.

Astonishingly, all of these attempts to escape paying for care take place while Americans pay more than any other country for health care. Americans now spend $8,233 per year per person. That figure is over two-and-a-half times more than most developed nations in the world, including relatively rich European countries like France, Sweden, and the United Kingdom.[12] The United States is one of the few industrialized nations where it is possible for medical bills to be the cause of personal bankruptcy. Some estimates claim 60 percent of the 1.5 million personal bankruptcies are due to unpaid medical bills.[13] Even for those lucky enough to be covered by employer-provided health insurance, reimbursement for catastrophic illness is something of a roll of the dice. The resulting bankruptcy does not merely affect the patient's finances. It is the doctors, hospitals, home health care providers, durable medical equipment suppliers, and others who remain unpaid.

In 1971, health care spending represented just 7.1 percent of GDP. In 2005, the figure was 16 percent. By 2012, health care spending accounted for 17.6 percent of everything the economy produced. (This figure also ignores those who require health care but simply do without.).
According to a 2005 CMS report,[14] 17 percent of health care spending was paid by taxpayers for Medicare; 16 percent was funded by taxpayers for Medicaid; taxpayers accounted for another 12 percent in school programs,

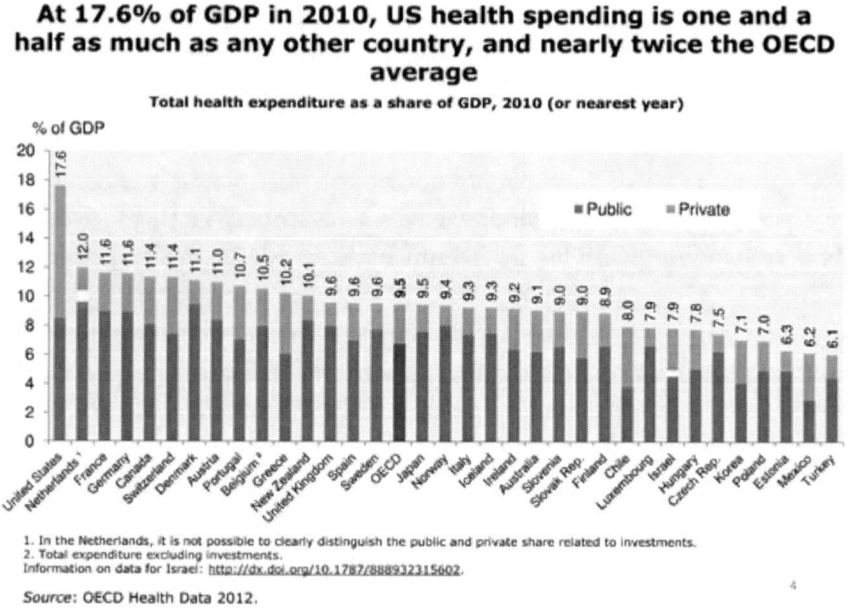

Figure 1.2

public hospitals, and veteran's programs; taxpayers' spending for government employees accounts for another 6 percent; private insurance covers 30 percent; patients pay out of pocket for 14 percent; and charity accounts for the final 5 percent.

ACA's Attempt to Address Health Care Fiscal Crisis

ACA is a remarkable piece of legislation which, in some small way, attempts to address many historical problems discussed in this chapter. While preserving the Medicare FFS model as far as the dollars will stretch, ACA attempts to preserve physician and participant autonomy, while eliminating "preexisting conditions" as a basis for denial of claims, increasing the number of healthy Americans who are contributing to the system.

ACA also attempts to reduce the number of uninsured in three important ways: (1) extending Medicaid coverage to persons earning less than 133 percent of the federal poverty level (FPL); (2) creating Health Insurance Marketplaces offering taxpayer subsidized private plans for individuals who are not offered coverage through work; and (3) enforcing the employer mandate, which requires larger employers to provide coverage or pay a penalty (although implementation has been delayed and may never come to pass) while providing tax incentives to smaller employers who provide coverage.

All of this comes at a cost. Between 2011 and 2013, health spending was projected to grow faster due to expected improvements in the economy, reaching a growth rate of 5.5 percent by 2013.[15] Private health insurance and out-of-pocket spending were both projected to grow faster over this period. Private health insurance spending was projected to grow 4.8 percent in 2013, up from 2.6 percent in 2010, as employer-sponsored insurance enrollment is expected to increase with gains in employment. Out-of-pocket spending was projected to grow 3.9 percent in 2013, up from 1.8 percent in 2010, as growth in household incomes is expected to lead to more health care spending and as employers are anticipated to increase cost-sharing requirements in employer-sponsored insurance plans.

In 2014, health spending is projected to grow 8.3 percent. This projected acceleration in the growth rate, up from 5.5 percent in 2013, is primarily the result of the ACA's coverage-related expansions. Medicaid eligibility is set to increase to persons under age 65 in families with income up to 133 percent of the federal poverty level in 2014. As a result, Medicaid enrollment is expected to increase by 19.5 million people, and spending is projected to grow 20.3 percent.

The new Health Insurance Marketplace is expected to cover 13.9 million people in 2014 and contribute to 9.4-percent growth in private health insurance spending. Because people gaining coverage through the Medicaid expansion and the Marketplace are expected to be younger and in better health than currently insured persons, on average, it is anticipated that a relatively higher share of their new costs would go toward physician and clinical services and prescription drugs and a lower share toward hospital and long-term care services.

Over the projection period (2010–2020), average annual health spending growth (5.8 percent) is anticipated to outpace average annual growth in the overall economy by 1.1 percentage points (4.7 percent). By 2020, national health spending is expected to reach $4.6 trillion and comprise 19.8 percent of GDP. The government-sponsored share of health spending is projected to increase from 45 percent in 2010 to about 50 percent by 2020, driven by expected robust Medicare enrollment growth, Medicaid coverage expansions, and Marketplace plan premium and cost-sharing subsidies.

How ACA Accountable Care Organizations and Shared Savings Programs Should Help

ACA authorized HHS to design a program that does not attempt to control how groups of providers manage to improve patient outcomes with limited funds. Instead, the Shared Savings Program (SSP) rewards both the reduction in costs and improvement in patient outcomes using various metrics to measure success. ACOs may choose to participate in one of two tracks:

Track 1: First (3-year) agreement period of one-sided shared savings, or
Track 2: First (3-year) agreement period of two-sided shared savings/losses

A one-sided shared savings agreement is one in which the ACO does not share risk of loss, while a two-sided shared savings agreement is one in which the ACO shares in savings and losses. One-sided risk model has a maximum share of savings of 50 percent for quality performance with a cap on shared savings at 10 percent. Two-sided risk model has a maximum share of savings of 60 percent for quality performance with a cap on shared savings at 15 percent. Track 1 is intended to provide an on-ramp for organizations to gain population management experience before transitioning to risk arrangements. Track 2 is intended for more sophisticated participants. All ACOs who elect to continue in the program after the first three-year agreement period must continue in the two-sided model. All ACOs share in the "first dollar" saved, once they meet or exceed Minimum Savings Rate.[16]

Accountable Care Organizations

According to CMS, ACOs grew out of the Dartmouth Atlas Project's work on geographic variations in cost and quality. [17] MedPAC featured the concept in its June 2009 report to Congress during the development of this health care reform provision. Congress drew from these expert sources as well as from the Physician Group Practice (PGP) demonstration project at CMS. On October 20, 2011, the Centers for Medicare & Medicaid Services (CMS), an agency within the Department of Health & Human Services (HHS), finalized new rules, 42 C.F.R. § 425.10 *et seq*. Under the Affordable Care Act, doctors, hospitals, and other health care providers are expected to better coordinate care for Medicare patients through ACOs. ACOs create incentives for health care providers to work together to treat an individual patient across care settings—including doctor's offices, hospitals, and long-term care facilities.

The Shared Savings Program

The Medicare Shared Savings Program will reward ACOs that lower their growth in health care costs while meeting performance standards on quality of care and putting patients first. Provider participation in an ACO is purely voluntary.[18] Section 3022 of the Affordable Care Act added a new section 1899 to the Social Security Act [19]that requires the Secretary to establish the Shared Savings Program. The rules for the program are at 42 C.F.R. § 425.10 *et seq*. This program is intended to encourage providers of services and suppliers (e.g., physicians, hospitals, and others involved in patient care) to create a new type of health care entity, an ACO, that agrees to be held accountable for improving the health and experience of care for individuals and improving the health of populations while reducing the rate of growth in health care spending. Studies have shown that better care often costs less, because coordinated care helps to ensure that the patient receives the right care at the right time, with the goal of avoiding unnecessary duplication of services and preventing medical errors.[20]

Section 1899(b) of the ACA Act establishes eligibility requirements for ACOs participating in the Shared Savings Program. Section 1899(b)(1) of the ACA Act allows several designated groups of providers of services and suppliers to participate as an ACO under this program, "as determined appropriate by the Secretary," and under the condition that they have "established a mechanism for shared governance." The statute lists the following groups of providers of services and suppliers as eligible to participate as an ACO:

- ACO professionals in group practice arrangements.
- Networks of individual practices of ACO professionals.
- Partnerships or joint venture arrangements between hospitals and ACO professionals.
- Hospitals employing ACO professionals.
- Such other groups of providers of services and suppliers as the Secretary determines appropriate.

An ACO provides an opportunity for Medicare beneficiaries to receive high-quality evidence-based health care that eliminates waste and reduces excessive costs through improved care delivery. However, there are significant differences between ACOs, as described in the final rule, and the private managed care plans offered under the Medicare Advantage program. ACOs are part of the traditional Medicare Fee-for-Service Program and beneficiaries continue to have the ability to choose any provider they choose.

The final rule, 42 C.F.R. § 425.10 *et seq.*,[21] calls for Medicare to assess the ACO's quality and financial performance based on a population's use of primary care services at the end of each year to determine whether a particular ACO should be credited with improving care and reducing growth in expenditures compared to a benchmark population. This means that an ACO has an incentive to improve the quality of care for all patients seen by its participating providers and suppliers.

The final rule defines an ACO as a group of providers and suppliers of services (e.g., hospitals, physicians, and others involved in patient care) that work together to coordinate care for the Medicare Fee-for-Service beneficiaries they serve. The goal of an ACO is to deliver seamless, high-quality care for Medicare beneficiaries, instead of the fragmented care that has so often been part of Fee-for-Service health care. The ACO will be a patient-centered organization where the patient and providers are true partners in care decisions.

ACOs that meet or exceed a minimum savings rate established under § 425.604 or § 425.606, meet the minimum quality performance standards established under § 425.500, and otherwise maintain their eligibility to participate in the Shared Savings Program under this part are eligible to receive payments for shared savings under subpart G.

The Shared Savings Program is a new approach to the delivery of health care aimed at reducing fragmentation, improving population health, and lowering overall growth in expenditures by

- promoting accountability for the care of Medicare fee-for-service beneficiaries,
- improving coordination of care for services provided under Medicare Parts A and B, and
- encouraging investment in infrastructure and redesigned care processes.[22]

Some Questions Remain with the Shared Savings Program

The basic idea is fairly straightforward: if a health care system or provider reduces total health care spending for its patients below the level that the payer (e.g., Medicare or a private health insurance plan) would have otherwise expected, the provider is rewarded with a portion of the savings. In a two-sided model, the participants also share in the failure to meet goals. At a macro level, the result is that CMS still spends less than it would have otherwise, and the provider gets more revenue than it would have otherwise expected. After the first three years, all SSPs will be two-way streets, with the system or provider sharing in the losses as well. Note too, the system could be compared to a game of chance which is played with "house money" and by "house rules"; chief among these, "the house always wins." Because the "expected" level is a variable controlled by government, which cannot afford to pay, critics are naturally concerned. Comments to the final rule also reveal distrust on the part of the public and providers. Others, such as the Center for Healthcare Quality and Payment Reform,[23] list concerns with the Shared Savings Program:

- *It Is Pay-for-Performance, not Fundamental Payment Reform.* Shared savings is just another form of pay-for-performance, without actually changing the current payment system at all. Where fees are too low to cover costs, a criticism often associated with Medicaid, ACOs would still lose money.

- *It Gives Providers Risk, without Providing Resources.* At first glance, shared savings looks like the perfect deal for the health care provider—if the provider is successful in reducing total costs, it gets a bonus. The logical flaw is in the assumption that there is no cost to the provider of doing what is needed to achieve success. The shared savings payment might ultimately cover those costs or it might not, and so the provider has no assurance that its increased costs will be covered.
- *It Rewards Historically High Spenders, Rather Than Low Spenders.* The communities and providers that have the most to gain from shared savings are the ones that historically use the most resources. In contrast, providers that are historically the nation's best performers—those with relatively low costs and high quality of care—are already "saving" Medicare and other payers significant amounts of money, but they receive no reward for doing what they have always done.
- *A Smaller Reduction in Revenue Is Still a Reduction.* In order for the payer (e.g., Medicare) to have any savings at all, some provider has to get less revenue than it would have otherwise received. If that provider is participating in the effort to reduce spending, giving them back an arbitrary share of the savings reduces the amount they lose, but they may still get less revenue than their actual cost of delivering services, which will discourage them from participating in the effort to create the savings in the first place.

Notes

1. ACA has not been completely codified into United States Code by the Office of the Law Revision Counsel (LRC). The "Pub. L. 111-148" citation means "111th Congress, 148th Public Law." Many provisions of ACA will eventually be assigned to a number of volumes of the United States Code, according to subject. For example,

those portions of ACA dealing with the False Claims Act have already been assigned to Title 31 of the United States Code, 31 U.S.C. §§ 3729–3733, while other provisions will likely be placed in some fashion in the Medicare section under Title 42. 42 U.S.C. § 1395. Even after inclusions in the United States Code, governmental bodies normally continue to refer to the section numbers appearing in the original Act, e.g., "Section 1899(b) of the Act."

2. http://www.cms.gov/Medicare/Medicare-Fee-for-Service-Payment/sharedsavingsprogram/Downloads/ACO-NarrativeMeasures-Specs.pdf.

3. http://www.cms.gov/Medicare/Medicare-Fee-for-Service-Payment/sharedsavingsprogram/Quality_Measures_Standards.html.

4. http://www.gpo.gov/fdsys/pkg/FR-2011–11–02/pdf/2011–27461.pdf.

5. Guy Carrin & Chris James, *Social Health Insurance: Key Factors Affecting the Transition towards Universal Coverage*, INT'L SOC. SECURITY REV., Jan. 2005, at 45–64.

6. Kaiser Family Foundation, http://facts.kff.org/chart.aspx?cb=58&sctn=168&ch=1785.

7. Medicaid General Information from the Centers for Medicare and Medicaid Services (CMS) website.

8. *National Federation of Independent Business v. Sebelius*, 132 S. Ct. 603 (2011).

9. DONALD BARTLETT & JAMES STEELE, CRITICAL CONDITION—HOW HEALTH CARE IN AMERICA BECAME BIG BUSINESS AND BAD MEDICINE (2004).

10. http://www.aapsonline.org/index.php/article/opt_out_medicare/.

11. http://oig.hhs.gov/compliance/physician-education/roadmap_web_version.pdf.

12. http://www.pbs.org/newshour/rundown/2012/10/health-costs-how-the-us-compares-with-other-countries.html.

13. http://www.cnn.com/2009/HEALTH/06/05/bankruptcy.medical.bills/.

14. Centers for Medicare and Medicaid Services, 2005 Report on National Health Expenditures, https://www.cms.gov/Research-Statistics-Data-and-Systems/Statistics-Trends-and-Reports/NationalHealthExpendData/downloads/tables.pdf (last accessed May 20, 2014).

15. "National Health Expenditures (NHE) in February 2014 grew 6.7% over February 2013." http://altarum.org/sites/default/files/uploaded-related-files/CSHS-Spending-Brief_April%202014.pdf (last accessed, May 20, 2014).

16. http://www.cms.gov/Medicare/Medicare-Fee-for-Service-Payment/sharedsavingsprogram/Downloads/ACO_Methodology_Factsheet_ICN907405.pdf.

17. ftp://ftp.cdc.gov/pub/CLIAC_meeting_presentations/pdf/Addenda/cliac0212/Tab_22_November_CLIAC_2012Feb15_ACO_Overview_Final_Rule.pdf.

18. http://www.cms.gov/Medicare/Medicare-Fee-for-Service-Payment/sharedsavingsprogram/Downloads/ACO_Summary_Factsheet_ICN907404.pdf.

20. http://www.cms.gov/Medicare/Medicare-Fee-for-Service-Payment/sharedsavingsprogram/Downloads/ACO_Summary_Factsheet_ICN907404.pdf.

21. Final Rule: 42 C.F.R. Part 425, 76 Fed. Reg. 67,802, *available at* http://www.gpo.gov/fdsys/pkg/FR-2011–11–02/pdf/2011–27461.pdf.

22. http://www.cms.gov/savingsprogram/.

23. http://www.chqpr.org/downloads/SharedSavings.pdf.

ARRA/HITECH/HIPAA and the Business Associate Agreement

2

"A covered entity's contract or other written arrangement with its business associate must contain the elements specified at 45 CFR 164.504(e)."

—U.S. Department of Health and Human Services[1]

Overview

When evaluating Business Associate Agreements to ensure compliance with the Final Rules of HIPAA and the HITECH Act, covered entities, business associates, and subcontractors should keep a fundamental question in mind—"For whom is an [Accountable Care Organization] ACO accountable?"[2] The answer is the patients. Congress embodied this notion in the Health Insurance Portability and Accountability Act of 1996 (HIPAA).[3] "Such guidelines shall include procedures to assure that such information is provided and utilized in a manner that appropriately protects the confidentiality of the information and the privacy of individuals receiving health care services and items."[4] These cornerstones of privacy and security in relation to a patient's medical record were subsequently reinforced in the passage of various regulations and the 2009 Health Information Technology for Economic and Clinical Health (HITECH) Act.[5] Hence, there is a nexus between the accountability of ACOs and HIPAA.

Just as the Centers for Medicare and Medicaid Services (CMS) established parameters for creating an ACO, the U.S. Department of Health and Human Services (HHS) implemented the final rule to "Modify the Health Insurance Portability and Accountability Act (HIPAA) Privacy, Security, and Enforcement Rules to implement statutory amendments under the Health Information Technology for Economic and Clinical Health Act ('the HITECH Act' or 'the Act') to strengthen the privacy and security protection for individuals' health information; modify the rule for Breach Notification for Unsecured Protected Health Information (Breach Notification Rule) under the HITECH Act to address public comment received on the interim final rule; . . . and make certain other modifications to the HIPAA Privacy, Security, Breach Notification, and Enforcement Rules (the HIPAA Rules) to improve their workability and effectiveness and to increase flexibility for and decrease burden on the regulated entities."[6] These Final Rules became effective on March 26, 2013, with a mandated compliance date of September 23, 2013 by covered entities, business associates, and subcontractors. A critical aspect of the initial proposed regulations and the final rule is the Business Associate Agreement (BAA).

The purpose of this chapter is to provide a brief history of the American Recovery and Reinvestment Act of 2009 (ARRA),[7] the HITECH Act, and HIPAA; define BAA, as well as some items to include in these agreements; and identify when a BAA should be used in the context of ACOs.

The History of ARRA/HITECH/HIPAA

HIPAA was passed in August 1996 in relation to the exposure of patients' protected health information (PHI). The Privacy Rule was issued on August 14, 2002, to protect individually identifiable health information.[8] And the Security Rule, issued on February 20, 2003, established national standards to guard PHI.[9]

In January 2005, a paradigm shift occurred in relation to HIPAA violations when the Department of Health and Human Services' Office of the Inspector General (OIG) issued *Supplemental Compliance Program Guidance for Hospitals.*[10] In relation to the HIPAA Privacy and Security Rules, the OIG indicated, "As of April 14, 2003, all hospitals that conduct electronic transactions for which standards have been adopted under the Health Insurance Portability and Accountability Act of 1996 (HIPAA) were required to comply with the Privacy Rule promulgated by HIPAA."[11] These regulations also reinforced that entities must be compliant with the Security Rule by April 20, 2005.[12]

Emphasis on protecting health information became more apparent. The Office of E-Health Standards and Services (OESS) was primarily created so that CMS could consolidate its HIPAA responsibilities and enforcement efforts.[13] In 2008, the OIG released a report after reviewing the oversight and enforcement of HIPAA activities by CMS from October 7, 2003, through August 24, 2007.[14] As of August 24, 2007, CMS had no proactive compliance review process, and during the audit, the OIG found significant vulnerabilities with "the hospitals' implementation of the administrative, technical, and physical safeguard provisions of the HIPAA Security Rule." These vulnerabilities have only become more apparent with Office for Civil Rights' (OCR) HIPAA Audit Pilot Program and the increase in HIPAA violations and HHS enforcement. Therefore, it is imperative that ACO participants execute BAAs when required and make certain that they contain the requisite elements.

What is a Business Associate Agreement?

A Business Associate Agreement (BAA) is "a covered entity's contract or other written arrangement with its business associate [that] must contain the elements specified at 45 CFR 164.504(e)."[15] Per the HIPAA Administrative Simplification regulations, a covered entity is a health care provider that "transmits any health information electronically in connection with a covered transaction, such as submitting health care claims to a health plan."[16] A hospital is considered a covered entity. Legal, actuarial, accounting, consulting, data aggregation, management, administrative, accreditation, or financial services fall under the HIPAA Rules' definition of a business associate, as "a person who performs functions or activities on behalf of, or certain services for, a covered entity that involved the use or disclosure of individually identifiable health information."[17] Subcontractors are those persons who store, handle, or transmit PHI either electronically or on paper and contract with the business associates. Covered entities, business associates, and subcontractors come under the purview of the HIPAA Final Rules. Therefore, it is imperative to execute these requisite agreements.

Like any contract, there are certain provisions that should be included in a BAA. First, an introduction that defines who the parties are, the parameters of the agreement, and the laws that are addressed. Oral contracts are not acceptable. HHS released guidance on what a BAA must stipulate in accordance with 45 C.F.R. §§ 164.502(e), 164.504(e), 164.532(d)–(e). These items include

- establishing the permitted and required uses of PHI;
- providing a non-disclosure provision;
- requiring assurances that the business associate or subcontractor will implement appropriate safeguards in keeping with the HIPAA Security Rule;
- requiring the report of a breach and use of PHI not provided for in the contract;
- requiring the business associate to ensure that any subcontractors it may engage on its behalf that will have access to protected health information agree to the same restrictions and conditions that apply to the business associate with respect to such information; and
- authorizing termination of the contract by the covered entity if the business associate violates a material term of the contract. Contracts between business associates and business associates that are subcontractors are subject to these same requirements.[18]

Other important provisions to include in a BAA are the scope, specific definitions (i.e., business associate, covered entity, and electronic protected health information), obligations and activities of the business associate, permitted uses and disclosures of the PHI, provisions for covered entities to inform a business associate of privacy practice and restrictions, permissible requests by a covered entity, term and termination, assurances, provision of a risk assessment, regulatory references, amendments, interpretation provision, breach notification protocol, and other relevant contractual provisions. Moreover, it is important to appreciate that a standard BAA should not be utilized. Certain subcontractors or business associates may have additional areas that need to be addressed, such as genetic information.

When Should a Business Associate Agreement Be Utilized in the Context of ACOs?

Whenever an entity is defined as a business associate contracting with a covered entity or a subcontractor contracting with a business associate, a BAA must be executed. Yet, there may be an option under the HIPAA Privacy Standards for multiple covered entities "to designate themselves as a single covered entity for purposes of compliance."[19] When multiple covered entities come under the umbrella of a single entity, Affiliated Covered Entity (ACE) status may be designated.[20] A critical factor is that the separate covered entities must be under common control or ownership.[21] The creation of an ACE must be documented and may be beneficial for an ACO that operates wholly owned subsidiaries.

Alternatively, an ACO might qualify as an Organized Health Care Arrangement (OHCA). In relation to HIPAA, an "OHCA can be either (1) a 'clinically integrated care setting in which individuals typically receive health care from more than one health care provider'; or (2) an organized system of healthcare in which the participating joint activities that include either utilization review, quality assessment and improvement activities related to the administration of risk sharing activities."[22] Hence, covered entities participating in an OCHA may disclose PHI to other OHCA participants in relation to the joint management and operations of the OHCA, as long as they are covered entities.

Another crucial area to consider in relation to BAAs is the scope of the function being performed by the covered entity. As part of their business operations, covered entities perform both covered and non-covered actions. For example, a health plan can process claims, which falls under the purview of a covered function, and conduct audits and other consultative functions, which are considered non-covered functions. The language in the Final Rules expressly illustrates this notion.

Many covered entities perform both covered and non-covered functions as part of their business operations. For such covered entities, the entire entity is generally required to comply with the Privacy Rule. However, the hybrid entity provisions of the HIPAA Rules permit the entity to limit the application of the Rules to the entity's components that perform functions that would make the component a "covered entity" if the component were a separate legal entity. Specifically, this provision allows an entity to designate a health care component by documenting the components of its organization that perform covered entity functions. The effect of such a designation is that most of the requirements of the HIPAA Rules apply only to the designated health care component of the entity and not to the functions the entity performs that are not included in the health care component. While most of the HIPAA Rules' requirements apply only to the health care component, the hybrid entity retains certain oversight, compliance, and enforcement obligations.

We explained in the preamble to the 2002 modifications to the Privacy Rule that the Rule provides hybrid entities with discretion as to whether or not to include business associate divisions within the health care component. However, a disclosure of protected health information from the health care component to any other division that is not part of the health care component, including a business associate division, is treated the same as a disclosure outside the covered entity. As a result, because an entity generally cannot have a business associate agreement with itself, a disclosure from the health care component to the business associate division(s) of the entity likely would require individual authorization.[23]

Importantly, after this final rule, business associates, by definition, are separately and directly liable for violations of the Security Rule and for violations of the Privacy Rule for impermissible uses and disclosures pursuant to their business associate contracts. With respect to a hybrid entity, however, not including business associate functions within the health care component of a hybrid entity could avoid direct liability and compliance obligations for the business associate component. Thus, we agree with the commenters that supported requiring inclusion of business associate functions inside the health care component of a hybrid entity. As such, the final rule requires that the health care component of a hybrid entity include all business associate functions within the entity.[24]

In order to avoid any gray area in terms of establishing "common control" or "common ownership" in relation to an ACE designation, it is best to execute a BAA, especially if a covered entity performs functions that are both covered and non-covered. Evaluating this risk now can mitigate the potential impact of non-compliance.

The Final Rule implements the proposed revisions to section 164.500. While we understand commenters' concerns regarding the uses and disclosures of health information by entities not covered by the Privacy Rule, the Department is limited to applying the HIPAA Rules to those entities covered by HIPAA (i.e., health plans, health care clearinghouses, and health care providers that conduct covered transactions) and to business associates, as provided under the HITECH Act.

As we discuss further below, section 13404 of the HITECH Act creates direct liability for impermissible uses and disclosures of protected health information by a business associate of a covered entity "that obtains or creates" protected health information "pursuant to a written contract or other arrangement described in § 164.502(e)(2)," and for compliance with the other privacy provisions in the HITECH Act. Section 13404 does not create direct liability for business associates with regard to compliance with all requirements under the Privacy Rule (i.e., does not treat them as covered entities). Therefore, under the final rule, a business associate is directly liable under the Privacy Rule for uses and disclosures of protected health information that are not in accord with its business associate agreement or the Privacy Rule.[25]

Since a covered entity, a business associate, and a subcontractor can be held liable for failing to execute a BAA, it is better to err on the side of caution. There is greater harm in transmitting PHI that does not conform to the rules than executing a BAA and alleviating any question as to the ACO's interactions qualifying as an ACE or an OHCA.

Conclusion

Business Associate Agreements are not new. Their execution between various entities has been required for years. The express language of direct liability for business associates and subcontractors coupled with the increased penalties promotes the notion of erring on the side of caution. Therefore, ACOs should closely evaluate their business structure, relationships with different entities, and whether or not they qualify as an ACE or meet all the components to be considered an OHCA. Being proactive can mitigate potential liability and give peace of mind to both the ACO participants and the patients they treat.

Notes

1. U.S. DEP'T OF HEALTH & HUMAN SERVS., HEALTH INFORMATION PRIVACY—BUSINESS ASSOCIATES, http://www.hhs.gov/ocr/privacy/hipaa/understanding/coveredentities/businessassociates.html.

2. Elliott Fisher, *Why Accountable Care? Core Principles Underlying ACOs*, BROOKINGS INST. 7 (June 7, 2010), https://xteam.brookings.edu/bdacoln/Documents/ACO%20Summit%20Fisher%20final%20%28June%207%202010%29.pdf.

3. Pub. L. No. 104-191.

4. H.R. REP. NO. 104-736, at 60 (1996) (Conf. Rep.), *reprinted in* 1996 U.S.C.C.A.N. 1990.

5. HITECH Act, Title XIII of Division A and Title IV of Division B of the American Recovery and Reinvestment Act of 2009, Pub. L. No. 111-5, 123 Stat. 226 (Feb. 17, 2009).

6. Modifications to the HIPAA Privacy, Security, Enforcement, and Breach Notification Rules under the Health Information Technology for Economic and Clinical

Health Act and the Genetic Information Nondiscrimination Act; Other Modifications to the HIPAA Rules; Final Rule, 78 Fed. Reg. 5,566 (Jan. 25, 2013).

7. Pub. L. No. 111-5 (2009).

8. 45 C.F.R. § 164.500—Applicability.

9. 45 C.F.R. § 164.302, .304.

10. 70 Fed. Reg. 4858 (Jan. 31, 2005), *available at,* http://oig.hhs.gov/fraud/docs/compliancguidance/012705HospSupplementalGuidance.pdf.

11. 67 Fed. Reg. 53181 (Aug. 14, 2002).

12. 68 Fed. Reg 8334 (Feb. 20, 2003).

13. Centers for Medicare and Medicaid Services, *Resources*, http://www.cms.gov/eHealth/about.html (last accessed May 20, 2014).

14. Department of Health and Human Services, Memorandum from The Office of the Inspector General, *Top Management and Performance Challenges in the Department of Health and Human Services for Fiscal Year 2008,* http://oig.hhs.gov/publications/challenges/files/TM_Challenges08.pdf (last accessed, May 20, 2014).

15. U.S. Dep't of Health & Human Servs., Health Information Privacy—Business Associates, http://www.hhs.gov/ocr/privacy/hipaa/understanding/coveredentities/businessassociates.html.

16. HIPAA Rules, 45 C.F.R. § 160.103.

17. U.S. Dep't of Health & Human Servs., OCR Privacy Brief, *Summary of the HIPAA Privacy Rule* 3 (2003) (http://www.hhs.gov/ocr/privacy/hipaa/understanding/summary/privacysummary.pdf) (explaining that persons or organizations do not qualify as business associates if their functions or services do not involve the use or disclosure of protected health information, and where any access to protected health information by such persons would be incidental, if at all).

18. A comprehensive list can be found at http://www.hhs.gov/ocr/privacy/hipaa/understanding/coveredentities/contractprov.html.

19. American Health Lawyers Association, Enterprise Risk Management Handbook for Healthcare Entities, 206–207 (2d ed. 2013).

20. 45 C.F.R. § 164.105(b).

21. 45 C.F.R. § 164.103 (providing that "common control" exists if an entity has the power, whether directly or indirectly, to materially influence or direct the actions or policies of another entity; "common ownership" is applicable if the equity interest in another covered entity is greater than or equal to 5%).

22. Amy Fehn, *The Importance of Health Information Technology for Accountable Care Organizations*, ABA HEALTH ESOURCE (June 2011) (citing 45 C.F.R. § 164.514 (referencing de-identified information as being that in which 18 identifiers that do not link a person to their medical record are removed) and 45 C.F.R. § 164.514 (indicating that de-identified information is no longer considered PHI)).

23. *See* 67 Fed. Reg. 53,182, 53,205 (Aug. 14, 2002).

24. 78 Fed. Reg. 5,566, 5,588 (Jan. 25, 2013).

25. *Id.* at 5,591.

3

Federal and State "Fraud and Abuse" Laws and Medical Ethics

The History of Fraud, Waste, and Abuse Laws

"Stark Law" is the name many physicians and providers assign to lump together both "Stark Law," 42 U.S.C. § 1395nn (enacted in 1989), and the "Anti-kickback Statute" (AKS), 42 U.S.C. § 1320a 7(b)(b) (1972). For the proper form see BB R 12.2.2(b). "Stark Law" is based largely upon AMA Code of Medical Ethics Opinions 8.03 "Conflicts of Interest in Patient Referrals," while the AKS is based upon Opinions 6.02–04 "Payments for Referrals," or "Fee Splitting."[1] This was no accident, as the federal government has always been careful to respect the Opinions of the AMA.

In order to understand why, one must consider that attempts at passage of the Medicare and Medicaid programs historically met with strong objections by the AMA;[2] principally upon fears the federal government would intrude upon "physician sovereignty"[3] as a gateway to unfettered socialism. On the other hand, from the federal perspective, regulation of physician behavior had always been a matter for state legislators and local medical boards. Congress likely felt it was giving little ground when it promised the AMA it would not interfere with the practice of medicine. The "Prohibition Against Any Federal Interference" law provides:

> Nothing in this subchapter shall be construed to authorize any Federal officer or employee to exercise any supervision or control over the practice of medicine or the manner in which medical services are provided, or over the selection, tenure, or compensation of any officer or employee of any institution, agency, or person providing health services; or to exercise any supervision or control over the administration or operation of any such institution, agency, or person.[4]

This as much as anything explains why the Affordable Care Act and the SSP I have no idea. Leave it to the governing body of the ACO to decide how best to accomplish objectives, as well as matters relating to compensation and distribution of savings and losses.

Medicare and Medicaid providers are nonetheless government contractors, and government contracts generally are subject to False Claims Act restrictions against overcharging the government or providing substandard goods and services. This has been true since the Civil War.[5] For over two centuries, it has been illegal to pay kickbacks for U.S. government contracts. In the case of physicians, the promise of non-interference could conceivably have been problematic. "Overcharging" the government could be synonymous with "overprescribing" treatment that might be medically unnecessary. This is the province of state medical boards. Only in the most extreme cases, usually based upon grossly excessive statistical evidence, has overtreatment been the subject of False Claims Act litigation.

However, federal statutes aimed at the financial circumstances that preceded the referral of the patient did not involve interfering with medical decisions. Indeed, since the AMA *itself* maintained a Code of Ethics declaring what financial entanglements sovereign physicians should avoid, it would be difficult for the AMA to object to its own rules. Thus, the AKS was enacted in 1972, followed by Stark Law in 1989, which largely codified AMA ethics. Though various changes have been made to federal law and the AMA Code of Ethics, the basic prohibitions taken from original AMA ethics rules have changed very little.

Various state statutes also exist, which have adopted AMA Ethics Opinions into state laws. California, Florida, Georgia, Massachusetts, New Jersey, North Carolina, and Texas all have a state version of the AKS.[6] As attention focuses upon the federal government's treatment and waiver of Federal fraud and abuse laws in relation to shared savings program waivers, one must not lose sight of the fact that federal waivers have no effect on AMA Ethics Opinions and state statutes that may still be enforced by state medical boards and state lawyers general. Rather than preempting these state laws, the federal government makes clear these laws continue unaffected. The federal fraud and abuse laws to which the federal waivers are addressed are as follows:

"Stark Law," the Physician Self-Referral Law (Section 1877 of the Social Security Act). Section 1877 of the Act (42 U.S.C. § 1395nn, the "Physician Self-Referral Law") is a civil strict liability statute that does not normally factor the intent of the parties. Stark Law prohibits physicians from making referrals for Medicare "designated health services," including hospital services, to entities with which they or their immediate family members have a financial relationship, unless an exception applies. These entities may not bill Medicare for services rendered as a result of a prohibited referral, and section 1877(g)(1) of the Act states that no payment may be made for a designated health service that is furnished pursuant to a prohibited referral.

The Federal anti-kickback statute (Section 1128B(b) of the Act). Section 1128B(b) of the Act (42 U.S.C. § 1320a–7b(b), the "Federal anti-kickback statute") provides criminal penalties for individuals or entities that knowingly and willfully offer, pay, solicit, or receive remuneration to induce or reward the referral of business reimbursable under any of the federal health care programs, as defined in section 1128B(f) of the Act. The offense is classified as a felony and is punishable by fines of up to $25,000 and imprisonment for up to 5 years. Violations of the Federal anti-kickback statute may also result in the imposition of civil monetary penalties (CMPs) under section 1128A(a)(7) of the Act (42 U.S.C. § 1320a–7a(a)(7)), program exclusion under section 1128(b)(7) of the Act (42 U.S.C. § 1320a–7(b)(7)), and liability under the False Claims Act (31 U.S.C. § 3729–33).

Prohibition on Inducements to Beneficiaries (Section 1128A(a)(5) of the Act). Section 28A(a)(5) of the Act (42 U.S.C. § 1320a–7a(a)(5), the "Beneficiary Inducements CMP") prohibits individuals and entities from offering or transferring remuneration to Medicare or Medicaid beneficiaries that the individual or entity knows or should know is likely to influence the beneficiary to order or receive from a particular provider, practitioner, or supplier any Medicare or Medicaid item or service. There are existing exceptions to the Beneficiary Inducements CMP at section 1128A(i)(6) of the Act.

Prohibition on Hospital Payments to Physicians to Induce Reduction or Limitation of Services (Sections 1128A(b)(1) and (2) of the Act). Sections 1128A(b)(1) and (2) of the Act (42 U.S.C. § 1320a–7a(b)(1)–(2), the "Gainsharing CMP") apply to certain payment arrangements between hospitals and physicians, including arrangements commonly referred to as "gainsharing" arrangements. Under section 1128A(b)(1) of the Act, a hospital is prohibited from making a payment, directly or indirectly, to induce a physician to reduce or limit services to Medicare or Medicaid beneficiaries under the physician's direct care. Hospitals that make (and physicians who receive) such payments are liable for CMPs of up to $2,000 per patient covered by the payments (sections 1128A(b)(1) and (2) of the Act).

Safe Harbors and Waivers of Fraud and Abuse Laws

Compensation arrangements between a hospital and a physician group, such as sharing achieved cost savings, would likely have violated the above federal Fraud and Abuse Laws as these types of arrangements did not meet the law's original safe harbors or exceptions. However, CMS and the OIG established the exemption in October 2011 that financial relationships between ACO participants are waived under the Stark Law if "reasonably related to the purposes of the [Medicare] Shared Savings Program."[7] Note, however, these waivers do not affect state versions of the AKS.

At the federal level, there are two methods of insulating an ACO and Shared Savings participants from Stark Law, the AKS, and the CMP law. First, a "safe harbor" under the Stark Law or AKS statute or regulation may protect the arrangement. These include "Stark Law" exceptions for employment, personal services arrangements, in-office ancillary services, electronic health records (EHR) arrangements, risk-sharing, and indirect compensation arrangements (to the extent an ACO arrangement is an indirect financial relationship).[8] Potential Federal anti-kickback statute safe harbors include those for employment, personal services and management contracts, EHR arrangements, and managed care arrangements.[9] Under the second method, a waiver may apply specifically to the ACO or shared savings program under the IFC Waiver published in the Federal Register.[10] Finding good cause to waive publication of a notice of proposed rulemaking, CMS and OIG (collectively, the Agencies) issued the Final ACO Waivers Rule as an interim final rule with comment period. However, there is a 60-day comment period, and the Agencies are required to consider comments and publish a final rule addressing those comments within three years.

An "ACO pre-participation" waiver of the Physician Self-Referral Law, the Federal anti-kickback statute, and the Gainsharing CMP that applies to ACO-related start-up arrangements in anticipation of participating in the Shared Savings Program, subject to certain limitations, including limits on the duration of the waiver and the types of parties covered. The regulations include:

- An "ACO participation" waiver of the Physician Self-Referral Law, the Federal anti-kickback statute, and the Gainsharing CMP that applies broadly to ACO-related arrangements during the term of the ACO's participation agreement under the Shared Savings Program and for a specified time thereafter;
- A "shared savings distributions" waiver of the Physician Self-Referral Law, Federal anti-kickback statute, and Gainsharing CMP that applies to distributions and uses of shared savings payments earned under the Shared Savings Program;
- A "compliance with the Physician Self-Referral Law" waiver of the Gainsharing CMP and the Federal anti-kickback statute for ACO arrangements that implicate the Physician Self-Referral Law and meet an existing exception; and
- A "patient incentive" waiver of the Beneficiary Inducements CMP and the Federal anti-kickback statute for medically related incentives offered by ACOs under the Shared Savings Program to beneficiaries to encourage preventive care and compliance with treatment regimes.

This interim final rule with comment period (IFC) establishes waivers of the application of the Physician Self-Referral Law, the Federal anti-kickback statute, and certain CMP law provisions to specified arrangements involving ACOs under section 1899 of the Social Security Act (the Act) (the Shared Savings Program), including ACOs participating in the Advance Payment Initiative. Section 1899(f) of the Act, as added by the Affordable Care Act, authorizes the Secretary of HHS to waive certain fraud and abuse laws as necessary to carry out the provisions of section 1899 of the Act. These regulations are effective on November 2, 2011.

State Laws Governing Physician Self-Referral and State Anti-kickback Laws

Statutes and regulations of each state may contain versions of Stark Law and the anti-kickback statute under various headings: "physician self-referral," "anti-kickback," "fee-splitting," "patient brokering," and other titles. State laws may regulate referrals involving publicly funded programs, like Medicaid, Medicare, TRICARE, and government employee programs, but frequently will also include referrals of patients who are covered by private insurance and self-funded plans, as well as cash-paying patients.

A full state-by-state treatment of these laws is beyond the scope of this book. The American Medical Association compiled a summary of these state laws, together with citation to the state codes where the laws can be found.[11] Always check the statutes and rules themselves, for the latest version of these laws.

State courts have struggled with the constitutionality of state versions of Stark law and the anti-kickback statute, particularly where the state statute does not contain "safe harbor" provisions as would be the case under the federal standard.[12] For this reason, many state statues will expressly incorporate the federal safe-harbors. Others may be subject to challenge for the reasons stated in *Harden*.

Reporting Requirements

ACOs that are seeking protection for one or more arrangements under the Medicare Shared Savings Program waivers related to application of the fraud and abuse laws have additional reporting requirements,[13] ACOs should continue to meet these disclosure requirements, as provided, until such time as additional guidance is issued specific to reporting for the Medicare Shared Savings Program waivers. ACOs that are seeking protection for one or more arrangements under certain of these waivers may use the same website described below to meet these disclosure requirements. Reporting must include the name of the ACO, the primary contact, composition, the names of the owners, participants, governing body and financial disclosures showing aggregate shared savings or losses, and how savings are distributed.[14]

The Problem Presented by ACOs and "Shared Savings" Programs

The IFC makes clear a waiver of a specific fraud and abuse law is not needed for an arrangement to the extent that the arrangement (1) does not implicate the specific fraud and abuse law or (2) implicates the law, but either fits within an existing exception or safe harbor, as applicable, or does not otherwise violate the law. Arrangements that do not fit in a waiver have no special protection and must be evaluated on a case-by-case basis for compliance with the Physician Self-Referral Law, the Federal anti-kickback statute, and the CMP laws.[15]

The shared savings waivers protect the activities of participants and providers that are "reasonably related" to ACO activities.[16] The question is, "What to do about everybody else?" Meaning, the patients who are not beneficiaries assigned to an ACO, and therefore any activities pertaining to them are necessarily unrelated to the ACO.

To illustrate, suppose members of the ACO are highly motivated to earn the shared savings reward. Assuming utmost good faith, the members honestly do their best to treat ACO patients ethically, but conservatively, in keeping with the spirit of the Affordable Care Act. Suppose further that physicians and hospitals forming the ACO also have a second set of patients who are covered by federal employee insurance, which often provides greater reimbursement than Medicare or Medicaid. It is easy to see the "Shared Savings" plan under the ACO actually creates a perverse incentive for the ACO physicians to conservatively treat the 5,000 ACO Medicare patients (because there are waivers) then possibly make up the difference through the cross-referral of other federally insured patients.

Simply put, there is a conflict of interest between shared savings program participants, who are on the one hand dividing up the ACO's shared savings losses and profits, and patients who on the other hand are non-ACO beneficiaries. Arrangements that do not fit in a waiver have no special protection and must be evaluated on a case-by-case basis for compliance with the Physician Self-Referral Law, the Federal anti-kickback statute, and the CMP laws.[17] Stark Law would likely prohibit outside referrals in this circumstance, due to the financial relationship of the shared savings participants. Even if this arrangement could arguably be considered included in the waiver because it is "reasonably related to the ACO" (it isn't), the AKS forbids payment in cash or "in kind" in exchange for referrals. Where participants are not being paid fair market value under the shared savings program (because there were losses), referrals between participants of other patients who are not ACO beneficiaries could be a felony under the federal AKS and various state laws that have adopted "illegal remuneration" statutes. Participants could be liable for tens of thousands of dollars in civil monetary penalties for each claim submitted.

AMA Ethics Opinions May Complicate Matters

While Stark Law and the AKS are derived from AMA Ethics Opinions, waiver of Stark Law and AKS restrictions have no effect on the continuing validity of AMA Ethics Opinions, which the federal government cannot waive. Stated another way, it is conceivable that a state medical board could ignore the federal waiver and determine that the Shared Savings arrangement is unethical under state law. In order to understand the risk, attention must focus upon the text of the Ethics Rules.

AMA Opinion 8.0321—Physicians' Self-Referral (Full Text)

Business arrangements among physicians in the health care marketplace have the potential to benefit patients by enhancing quality of care and access to health care services. However, these arrangements can also be ethically challenging when they create opportunities for self-referral in which patients' medical interests can be in tension with physicians' financial interests. Such arrangements can undermine a robust commitment to professionalism in medicine as well as trust in the profession.

In general, physicians should not refer patients to a health care facility that is outside their office practice and at which they do not directly provide care or services when they have a financial interest in that facility. Physicians who enter into legally permissible contractual relationships—including acquisition of ownership or investment interests in health facilities, products, or equipment; or contracts for service in group practices—are expected to uphold their responsibilities to patients first. When physicians enter into arrangements that provide opportunities for self-referral they must:

(1) Ensure that referrals are based on objective, medically relevant criteria.

(2) Ensure that the arrangement:

(a) is structured to enhance access to appropriate, high quality health care services or products; and

(b) within the constraints of applicable law:

(i) does not require physician-owners/investors to make referrals to the entity or otherwise generate revenues as a condition of participation;

(ii) does not prohibit physician-owners/investors from participating in or referring patients to competing facilities or services; and

(iii) adheres to fair business practices vis-à-vis the medical professional community—for example, by ensuring that the arrangement does not prohibit investment by nonreferring physicians.

(3) Take steps to mitigate conflicts of interest, including:

(a) ensuring that financial benefit is not dependent on the physician-owner/investor's volume of referrals for services or sales of products;

(b) establishing mechanisms for utilization review to monitor referral practices; and

(c) identifying or if possible making alternate arrangements for care of the patient when conflicts cannot be appropriately managed/mitigated.

(4) Disclose their financial interest in the facility, product, or equipment to patients; inform them of available alternatives for referral; and assure them that their ongoing care is not conditioned on accepting the recommended referral.

AMA Ethics Opinion 8.051—Conflicts of Interest under Capitation (Full Text)

The application of capitation to physicians' practices can result in the provision of cost-effective, quality medical care. It is important to note, however, that the potential for conflict exists under such systems. Physicians who contract with health care plans should attempt to minimize these conflicts and to ensure that capitation is applied in a manner consistent patients' interests.

(1) Physicians have an obligation to evaluate a health plan's capitation payments prior to contracting with that plan to ensure that the quality of patient care is not threatened by inadequate rates of capitation. Physicians should advocate that capitation payments be calculated primarily on the basis of relevant medical factors, available outcomes data, the costs associated with involved providers, and consensus-oriented standards of necessary care. Furthermore, the predictable costs resulting from existing conditions of enrolled patients should be considered when determining the rate of capitation. Different populations of patients have different medical needs and the costs associated with those needs should be reflected in the per member per month payment. Physicians should seek agreements with plans that provide sufficient financial resources for all care that is the physician's obligations to deliver and should refuse to sign agreements that fail in this regard.

(2) Physicians must not assume inordinate levels of financial risk and should therefore consider a number of factors when deciding whether or not to sign a provider agreement. The size of the plan and the time period over which the rate is figured should be considered by physicians evaluating a plan as well as in determinations of the per member per month payment. The capitation rate for large plans can be calculated more accurately than for smaller plans because of the mitigating influence of probability and the behavior of large systems. Similarly, length of time will influence the predictability of the cost of care. Therefore, physicians should advocate for capitation rates calculated for large plans over an extended period of time.
(3) Stop-loss plans can prevent the potential of catastrophic expenses from influencing physician behavior. Physicians should ensure that such arrangements are finalized prior to signing an agreement to provide services in a health plan.
(4) Physicians must be prepared to discuss with patients any financial arrangements which could impact patient care. Physicians should avoid reimbursement systems that, if disclosed to patients, could negatively affect the patient-physician relationship.

State Fraud and Abuse Laws

Each individual state may have enacted laws and administrative regulations which must be considered in conjunction with federal laws and ethics decisions. Some states, such as Florida, are quite expansive. Others may be less so. The American Health Lawyers Association maintains a state survey of Fraud and Abuse laws for all 50 states.[18] As with any third-party source, it is important to update the research to ensure that you have the most current set of statues and regulations.

Conclusion

Stark Law, the AKS, and the federal fraud and abuse regulations have to some degree adopted the most up-to-date provisions of AMA Ethics Opinions, but federal waiver of "conflict of interest" laws such as Stark Law cast a favorable an eye toward that which saves the government money, ethics notwithstanding.

Ethically, this leads to a startling conclusion: A very strong argument could be made that the AMA Code and state AKS statutes would preclude Shared Savings Programs. Patients are being charged a "hidden tax," as described in a recent Florida State University College of Social Sciences and Public Policy article. In the article, Kate Franzese cogently explains why the entire system couldn't pass an ethics test:

> Medicare and Medicaid have been around since the mid-twentieth century, but these publicly funded health programs are not without their flaws. While they have produced a few meritorious results, such as reducing the number of uninsured Americans, several other less-than-desirable secondary effects have emerged from this socialized medical system. Perhaps the most visible concern now is the underpayment of physicians and insurance companies. Medical professionals often cannot bill Medicare and Medicaid patients for the full cost of services delivered. Thus, they are forced to charge higher prices to other (unsubsidized) patients. Underpayment for services decreases the incentives for doctors to treat Medicare and Medicaid patients. Ultimately, patients suffer from the ramifications of healthcare policy's unintended side effects.
>
> One such effect is the so-called "hidden tax" Medicare and Medicaid impose on unsubsidized patients (i.e., those not on a public health insurance program). When Medicare or Medicaid patients are treated they are compensated based on a schedule of fess set by the government. Health care professionals are commonly paid less than the value of the services they provide. Thus, the only way to compensate for the difference is by increasing costs to other, non-subsidized patients. The more people covered by Medicare, the larger

> gap between providers' costs and the payments they receive, which increases costs to anyone privately insured. The "hidden tax" is the extra money paid by nonsubsidized patients to cover the gap between the actual cost of services provided and the fees paid by the government.[19]

It remains to be seen whether there will be challenges to the Shared Savings Program at the local level, or if these concerns are merely academic.

Notes

1. According to the AMA website, "For more than 165 years, the Code of Medical Ethics has been the authoritative ethics guide on medical professionalism. The Code speaks to the enduring values of medicine as a profession. As a statement of the values to which physicians commit themselves individually and collectively, the Code is the standard for medicine as a professional community." The AMA Code is not law, unless a particular state or judicial opinion has adopted a provision of the code as such. More commonly, in an administrative hearing or lawsuit on this issue of "ethics," an expert witness will base his or her opinion upon the AMA Code as being the accepted standard of care. Available at http://www.ama-assn.org//ama/pub/physician-resources/medical-ethics/code-medical-ethics.page.

2. In fact, the AMA went so far as to hire then-actor Ronald Reagan to record the 10-minute phonograph "Ronald Reagan Speaks Out against Socialized Medicine," which warned of all manner of imminent danger of medical imposition of socialism as a gateway to a government takeover of private enterprise. The phonograph can be viewed at http://www.youtube.com/watch?v=fRdLpem-AAs.

3. PAUL STARR, THE SOCIAL TRANSFORMATION OF AMERICAN MEDICINE: THE RISE OF A SOVEREIGN PROFESSION AND THE MAKING OF A VAST INDUSTRY (Basic Books 1982). Winner of the 1983 Pulitzer Prize, Starr tells how the entire American health care system of doctors, hospitals, health plans, and government programs has evolved over the last two centuries.

4. 42 U.S.C. § 1395.

5. 31 U.S.C. § 3729–33.

6. In Texas, for example, the Texas Illegal Remuneration Act mirrors the Federal anti-kickback prohibition but expands the prohibition to cover items and services reimbursed by any payer (including self-payers), rather than just federally funded health plans. Thus, in Texas, the anti-kickback prohibition applies in situations involving all reimbursable health care items or services. *See* W. MARC MCDONALD & KAMI K. BEATY, LEGAL ISSUES AFFECTING PHYSICIAN RECRUITMENT ARRANGEMENTS, http://www.bwwlaw.com/downloads/wmm/Physician_Recruitment_Paper.pdf.

7. *See* Final Waivers in Connection with the Shared Savings Program, 76 Fed. Reg. 67,992–68,010; Medicare Program; Medicare Shared Savings Program: Accountable Care Organizations, 76 Fed. Reg. 67,802–990.

8. Stark Law Statutory Safe Harbors, 42 U.S.C. § 1395nn; Code of Federal Regulation Safe Harbors, 42 C.F.R. § 411.357.

9. ASK Safe Harbors, 42 C.F.R. § 1001.952.

10. *See* Final Waivers in Connection with the Shared Savings Program and Medicare Program; Medicare Shared Savings Program: Accountable Care Organizations, *supra* note 7.

11. http://www.ama-assn.org/resources/doc/clrpd/self-referral-laws.pdf

12. *See State v. Harden*, 873 So.2d 352 (Fla. 2004)("At first glance, section 409.920(2)(e), Florida Statutes (2000), appears to track the language of the federal statute," upon closer inspection, the statute lacks a "knowing" or "Willful" element, and does not contain a "safe harbor." The court held the statute unconstitutional.)

13. 76 Fed. Reg. 68000–1. Guidance related to these additional reporting requirements is contained in the Final Waivers in Connection with the Shared Savings Program interim final rule, 76 Fed. Reg. 67992, 68004–5. ACO Public Reporting Guidance, CTRS. FOR MEDICARE & MEDICAID SERVS. (Dec. 17, 2012), http://www.cms.gov/Medicare/Medicare-Fee-for-Service-Payment/sharedsavingsprogram/ACO-Public-Reporting-Guidance.html.

14. Centers for Medicare and Medicaid Services, *Medicare Shared Savings Program Interaction with the Physician Quality Reporting System (PQRS)*, http://www.cms.gov/Medicare/Medicare-Fee-for-Service-Payment/sharedsavingsprogram/Downloads/PQRS-FAQs.pdf (last accessed, May 20, 2014).

15. Interim Final Rule, 76 Fed. Reg. 67,992–68,010.

16. Interim Final Rule, *supra* note 12.

17. Interim Final Rule, *supra* note 12.

18. http://www.healthlawyers.org/Members/PracticeGropus/FA/Surveys/Pages/FiftyStateSurvey.aspx.

19. *See* Kate Franzese, *Will Obamacare's "Hidden Tax" Limit Health Care Access?*, DEVOE L. MOORE CENTER (Feb. 12, 2013), http://www.coss.fsu.edu/dmc/content/will-obamacares-hidden-tax-limit-health-care-access.

4 ACOs Accountable Care Organizations and Respondeat Superior

Let the chief answer. A superior is responsible for any acts of omission or commission by a person of less responsibility to him.

—Black's Law Dictionary

Overview

Accountable Care Organizations (ACOs) encompass a variety of combinations of entities. For example, an ACO can consist of relationships between "integrated systems, hospitals with aligned practices, physician groups/networks, [or] community health systems."[1] ACOs may or may not participate in the Medicare Shared Savings Program, depending on whether or not they meet the requirements.[2] As established by section 3022 of the Affordable Care Act (ACA), several criteria must be met in order for the Centers for Medicare and Medicaid Services (CMS) to approve the arrangement.[3] For example, some of the requisite criteria include[4]

- accountability to the assigned Medicare fee-for-service beneficiaries in terms of quality, cost, and overall care;
- execution of an agreement for a three-year minimum;
- creation of a formal legal structure;

- establishment of a leadership and management structure that incorporates both clinical and administrative components; and
- utilization of various technologies to coordinate care and to report various clinical and cost measures.

Of these criteria, the component most relevant to ACOs in relation to respondeat superior is the legal structure. The chosen structure defines the interactions between the organizations and the individuals involved in them. Therefore, the purpose of this chapter is to define respondeat superior, provide context for the doctrine, and apply how ACOs are impacted.

What Is Respondeat Superior?

The U.S. Supreme Court adopted the Restatement (Third) of Agency, which defines respondeat superior liability, whereby "an employer is subject to liability for torts committed by employees while acting within the scope of their employment."[5] Alternatively, the Court distinguished respondeat superior liability from supervisory liability and indicated that "[e]ven if an employer is not liable for the actions of his employee solely because the employee was acting within the scope of employment, there still might be conditions to render a supervisor liable for the conduct of his subordinate."[6] Multiple tests have been utilized to discern supervisory liability, including:

- actual knowledge of a subordinate's conduct;
- a supervisor's "know[ledge] about the conduct and [whether or not to] facilitate it, approve it, condone it, or turn a blind eye for fear of what they might see"; or
- no actual knowledge to do recklessness or gross negligence.[7]

By way of analogy, *United States and Wisconsin ex rel. Keltner v. Lakeshore Medical Clinic, Ltd.*[8] is illustrative of the concept of respondeat superior and, alternatively, supervisory liability in the context of self-audit results and the impact on compliance and liability. Here, a former employee under the False Claims Act and similar state law, alleging that fraudulent Medicare and

Medicaid payment claims had been filed for Evaluation and Management Codes (E/M) services, sued a large medical group. Specifically, an internal audit had been conducted that revealed that two physicians had "up-coded" more than 10 percent of their respective claims. While the identified claims were reported and returned to the government, the non-audited claims were not and the code review process was terminated by the practice. Given the court's decision, the employee and the government may proceed with their claims, having overcome the motion to dismiss. Hence, if the physicians were employees or partners, respondeat superior would apply. Alternatively, supervisory liability may attach because the supervisors made a decision to ignore the findings and continue to submit "up-coded" claims.

It is crucial to recognize that respondeat superior liability always looms as the next section demonstrates.

The Traditional Application of Respondeat Superior

Common areas associated with respondeat superior include hospital liability for injuries caused by employees, liability for injuries caused by physicians or employees acting under their supervision, and corporate responsibility.[9] Stemming back to 1914, Justice Benjamin Cardozo addressed respondeat superior in the context of a negligent act and the liability relationship between a hospital and a physician. The sentiment of the time was that physicians were not employees and a hospital's responsibility was solely for negligent acts of its employees, such as nurses.[10] Hence, respondeat superior would apply to a hospital if a nurse negligently carried out a physician's order, but the physician would not have been liable in this instance in the 1920s.

The trend of separating the acts of physicians, whether employees or independent contractors, began to shift as the business of providing care changed.[11] The ability to no longer insulate actions of hospitals from physicians is espoused by the Kentucky Supreme Court in dicta that "the historical view of hospitals as hotels providing rooms, building where private medical practitioners treat private patients . . . is no longer viable."[12] This notion opened the doors for respondeat superior to apply liability to a hospital—or an ACO—for negligent acts of individuals associated with the entity. Two cases applying different state laws highlight this notion.

In *Cahill v. HCA Management Company*,[13] the patient allegedly sustained injuries when a medical technician negligently performed a venipuncture. The trial court entered a directed verdict in favor of the management corporation and the patient appealed. The Fourth Circuit Federal Court of Appeals vacated the judgment and remanded the case to the District Court for further proceedings because North Carolina "subscribes to the axiom that the right of supervision and control imposes vicarious liability on a principal for the negligent acts of its agent committed within the scope of his employment."[14] Under the doctrine of respondeat superior, the litmus test for liability is the power of control, which highlights the notion that a "servant can have two masters."[15] Interestingly, this case involved HCA Management Company (HMC), a subsidiary of Hospital Corporation of America. Here, Ashe Memorial Hospital and HMC entered into a contractual agreement whereby HMC was responsible for "[t]he hiring, discharge, supervision and management of all employees of the hospital, including the determination of the numbers and qualifications of employees needed . . . ," while Ashe Memorial trustees retained "full authority and ultimate control over the hospital."[16] Ultimately, the court held that while the contract between HMC and Ashe Memorial Hospital might have an indemnity provision, because of the degree of control that HMC exercised, the patient was able to recover based on state common law. This type of liability, which stems from a contractual relationship and clinical care performance, should be considered in the context of ACOs.

A second example stems from the Ohio Supreme Court in *Taylor v. Belmont Community Hospital*, where the issue on appeal was "whether the medical negligence action filed against the employer hospital for respondeat superior liability could proceed even though no suit had been filed against the employee physician or the two employee nurses and where the statute of limitations had expired against these allegedly primarily liable parties."[17] In this instance, a patient went to a hospital emergency room for a simple x-ray of her knee. During the course of treatment, she was dropped by two hospital employees and required two surgeries and subsequent nursing care. Mrs. Taylor, her husband, and the Ohio Department of Job and Family

Services filed a complaint against the hospital alleging negligence. In applying the doctrine of respondeat superior, whereby "an employer or principal is vicariously or secondarily liable for the negligence of its employee or agent, whose liability is primary."[18] Because of the employer-employee relationship, the court applied respondeat superior and subsequently reversed and remanded the case to the trial court.

Persons affiliated with ACOs should take care to consider the context of the legal structure and the subsequent relationships that are created. Depending on various state laws and ownership interests, respondeat superior, supervisory liability, and vicarious liability may apply.

How Are ACOs Impacted by the Doctrine of Respondeat Superior?

Just as hospitals are required by The Joint Commission to establish an organized governing body with individuals who create policy, ensure clinical quality standards, and execute management and planning, section 3022 of ACA requires ACOs to create a legal entity, which has both clinical and administrative components.[19] As the Commonwealth Fund illustrated, there are different ways to structure ACOs; however, regardless of the legal structure, respondeat superior is always a consideration.[20] Respondeat superior (e.g., vicarious liability or imputed negligence) assigns liability on a seemingly "blameless" person for another's negligence based upon the relationship.[21] Meaning that if a physician, as a direct employee or an agent, whether express, implied, or ostensible, acts negligently, the hospital can incur liability, too.

The following examples of ACOs highlight the notion of considering the state law, structure, and physician compensation model in relation to respondeat superior.[22]

ACO Entity	Structure/ Governance	Programs	Payment Model with Payer	Physician Compensation Model
Accountable Care Alliance (Omaha, Neb.)	Limited liability organization created by two hospital systems and three physician groups.	Commercial.	Initially only shared savings.	Three potential models: (1) full employment, (2) contracts with performance standards, or (3) independent physicians with common protocols.
Arizona Connected Care (Tucson, AZ)	Limited liability company—physician-led partnership with TMC Healthcare System.	Medicare Shared Savings Program (SSP), commercial, and Medicaid SSP.	Shared savings with expectation to adopt downside risk later.	75 percent of savings shared with PCP, specialists, and hospital based on patient volume and quality of care.
Cheyenne ACO (Cheyenne, WY)	Limited liability—50-50 partnership between physician group and CRMC.	Delaying Medicare SSP application for one year.	Medicare risk models under consideration.	To be determined.
MACIPA Pioneer ACO (Cambridge, MA)	No joint legal structure—IPA and hospital negotiate payer contracts jointly.	Medicare Advantage, commercial plans, Medicare Pioneer.	Upside and downside risk arrangements.	Physicians receive fee for service.

As the chart indicates, there are many different ways to structure ACOs, which have varying degrees of impact on respondeat superior liability. First, an entity should always turn to the state law, which governs the contract and legal structure. Second, members of a hospital's medical staff and ACO may or may not be employees. So, "[i]f a hospital is a member of a newly formed ACO, its MS members may seek ACO membership as a complement to their hospital-based clinical privileges in order to increase their income."[23] But both parties need to be aware that employing medical staff creates the situation where the physician is "serving two masters—the ACO and the hospital"—in tandem.[24] Hence, creating liability under respondeat superior.

Liability consequences may arise in a multitude of scenarios, including

- malpractice;
- nonperformance and breach of contractual duties and obligations; and
- physician employment termination may result in wrongful termination.[25]

These potential legal pitfalls may be minimized by considering the ramifications of state and federal laws and regulations, due process hearings,[26] and arbitration and/or mediation clauses. Because there are multiple areas of vulnerability potentially impacting the liability of the ACO and the participants, respondeat superior cannot be ignored.

Conclusion

While the implementation of ACOs is in its infancy, the doctrine of respondeat superior is akin to an octogenarian. It has been around for many years and has undergone a broader application as other areas of law and health care industry dynamics change. Therefore, it is incumbent upon persons entering into ACOs to consider the potential scenarios that give rise to the doctrine of respondeat superior. Being proactive can mitigate costly and potentially adverse legal consequences in the future.

Notes

1. Elliott Fisher, *Why Accountable Care? Core Principles Underlying ACOs*, Brookings Inst. 7 (June 7, 2010), https://xteam.brookings.edu/bdacoln/Documents/ACO%20Summit%20Fisher%20final%20%28June%207%202010%29.pdf.

2. Sharon Silow-Carroll & Jennifer Edwards, Commonwealth Fund, Early Adopters of the Accountable Care Model: A Field Report on Improvements in Health Care Delivery 10 (Sandra Hackman ed., Mar. 2013).

3. The Affordable Care Act, Pub. L. No. 111-148 124 stat. 896(Mar. 11, 2010) (adding section 3022, Medicare Shared Savings Program, and amending title XVIII of the Social Security Act, 42 U.S.C. § 1395 *et seq*., through the addition of section 1899, 42 U.S.C. § 1395jjj). The proposed rules were implemented on March 31, 2011, by CMS, which implemented the ACO provision of ACA, which is considered an element of the Medicare Shared Savings Program. 76 Fed. Reg. 19,528 (Apr. 7, 2011). Subsequently, the final rules were released on October 20, 2011, and published in the November 2, 2011, *Federal Register*. 76 Fed. Reg. 67,802 (Nov. 2, 2011).

4. Stephen E. Ronai, *The Patient Protection and Affordable Care Act's Accountable Care Organization Program: New Healthcare Disputes and the Increased Need for ADR Services*, DISP. RESOL. J., August/October 2011, at 3 (citing Julie Kass et al., *CMS Proposal Provides Framework for ACO and Shared Savings Program Rules*, 9 HEALTH L. NEWS (2011)).

5. Ashcroft v. Iqbal, 129 S. Ct. 1937, 1958 (2009) (adopting RESTATEMENT (THIRD) OF AGENCY § 2.04 (2005)). Although not a health care case, *Iqbal* is a seminal case on a variety of legal issues. Factually, a pretrial detainee brought a claim against various government officials alleging a multitude of unconstitutional actions.

6. *Id.* at 1958 (referring to Whitfield v. Melendez-Rivera, 431 F.3d 1, 14 (1st Cir. 2005) to delineate between respondeat superior and supervisory liability).

7. *Id.* at 1958 (citing Baker v. Monroe Twp., 50 F.3d 1186, 1194 (3d Cir. 1995); Int'l Action Ctr. v. United States, 365 F.3d 20, 28 (D.C. Cir. 2004); Lipsett v. Univ. of P.R., 864 F.2d 881, 902 (1st Cir. 1988)).

8. *United States and Wisconsin, ex rel. Keltner v. Lakeshore Med. Clinic, Ltd.*, Case No. 11-cv-00892 (E.D. Wis. Mar. 28, 2013).

9. Todd Lard, Comment, *A Symposium on Film and the Law:* Strubhart v. Perry Memorial Hospital*: Oklahoma Adopts Hospital Corporate Liability*, 22 OKLA. CITY U. L. REV. 451 (1997) (examining respondeat superior in terms of inadequate treatment and a hospital's corporate responsibility to ensure that medical staff is competent as an independent duty).

10. Schoendorff v. Soc'y of N.Y. Hosp., 105 N.E. 92, 94 (N.Y. 1914).

11. D.H. Rutchik, *The Emerging Trend of Corporate Liability: Courts' Uneven Treatment of Hospital Standards Leaves Hospitals Uncertain and Exposed*, 47 VAND. L. REV. 535, 537 (1994).

12. Paintsville Hosp. Co. v. Rose, 683 S.W.2d 255, 258 (Ky. 1985).

13. 812 F.2d 170 (4th Cir. 1987).

14. *Id.* at 171 (citing Azzolino v. Dingfelder, 322 S.E.2d 567, 586–589 (1984)).

15. *Id.* at 171.

16. *Id.* at 170.

17. *Taylor v. Belmont Community Hosp.*, 2010 WL 3328650, at *1. 7th Dist. No. 090BE30, 2010-Ohio-3986.

18. *Id.* at *2 (citing Clark v. Southview Hosp. & Family Health Ctr., 68 Ohio St. 3d 435 (1994)).

19. *See* Ronai, *supra* note 4; JOINT COMMISSION, COMPREHENSIVE ACCREDITATION MANUAL FOR HOSPITALS: INTRODUCTION TO THE LEADERSHIP STRUCTURE, STANDARDS LD.01.01.01–LD.01.07.01 (2011) ("Many leadership responsibilities directly affect the provision of care, treatment, and services, as well as the day-to-day operations of the hospital. In some cases, these responsibilities will be shared among leadership groups, and in other cases, a particular leader or leadership group has primary responsibility. Regardless of the hospital's structure, it is important that leaders carry out all their responsibilities.").

20. SILOW-CARROLL & EDWARDS, *supra* note 2.

21. *See* W. PAGE KEETON ET AL., PROSSER AND KEETON ON THE LAW OF TORTS § 70, at 500 (5th ed. 1984).

22. SILOW-CARROLL & EDWARDS, *supra* note 2, at 12–13 (illustrating key characteristics and activities of seven ACOs in a comprehensive chart).

23. Ronai, *supra* note 4, at 5.

24. *Id.*

25. *Id.*

26. *See* Healthcare Quality Improvement Act, 42 U.S.C. § 11112 (requiring "due process" notice and hearing standards for ACO sanctions based on professional review). Additionally, the ACO's sanctions could trigger the requirement that the noncompliant ACO physician be reported under 42 U.S.C. § 11135(a) to the National Practitioner Data Bank.

Antitrust Matters

5

"We all need to cast our stereotypes aside and to approach each other—not as regulators and regulated, not as doctors and lawyers and patients—but as Americans who all want to realize the potential of ACOs to spark true health care reform."

—Jon Leibowitz, Former FTC Chairman[1]

As this book covers several aspects of Accountable Care Organizations (ACOs) and is intended for a broader audience than just antitrust practitioners, it is worth exploring the evolution of the relevant antitrust laws, major cases, and enforcement activities. To this end, this chapter will begin by reviewing antitrust agencies and principles and then move to the application of the prevailing doctrines and recent agency guidance related to health care joint ventures and ACOs in particular.

Enforcement Agencies and Private Parties

The Federal Trade Commission (FTC) and Department of Justice (DOJ) Antitrust Division (together, the "Agencies") are the federal agencies primarily responsible for the enforcement of antitrust laws impacting the health care sector. Accordingly, much of the discussion in this chapter is devoted to their guidance, advisory opinions, and enforcement activities. The FTC's goal is "to prevent business practices that are anticompetitive or deceptive or unfair to consumers; to enhance informed consumer choice and public understanding of the competitive process; and to accomplish this without unduly burdening legitimate business activity."[2] The FTC brings civil enforcement actions through its Bureau of Competition. The bureau has a Health Care Division with approximately 35 lawyers and investigators who work on health care antitrust matters exclusively.[3] The DOJ's Antitrust Division "promote[s] economic competition through enforcing and providing guidance on antitrust laws and principles."[4] The DOJ brings both civil actions and criminal suits to enforce federal antitrust laws.

Except for the laws in which enforcement action is reserved to a specific federal agency or where the courts have held no private right of action exists, states and private parties may sue to enforce federal and state antitrust laws. A majority of antitrust lawsuits, often merger related, are brought by businesses and individuals seeking monetary damages or injunctions under the Sherman Antitrust and Clayton Acts.[5] These cases may also involve credentialing matters, such as a physician being denied privileges by a hospital or peer-review committee for anticompetitive reasons.[6]

Overview of Relevant Antitrust Laws

Section 1 of the Sherman Antitrust Act[7] prohibits agreements that unreasonably restrain competition.[8] In the health care context, this will generally deal with horizontal agreements between two or more competitors. Violations of the Sherman Act may involve civil or criminal penalties. The DOJ, state lawyers general, and private parties may sue to enforce the civil provisions of the Sherman Act, while only the DOJ can enforce its criminal provisions. Individuals can be fined up to $1 million and sentenced up to 10 years in federal prison for each offense, while corporations can be fined up to $100 million for each offense. Under certain circumstances, these fines may be increased.

Section 5(a) of the Federal Trade Commission Act[9] prohibits unfair methods of competition in or affecting commerce.[10] The FTC has used section 5 of the FTC Act as the basis for enforcing violations of the Sherman Act. The courts have held that the FTC is the only agency with the authority to bring suit under the FTC Act and that no private right of action exists.[11] Violations of the FTC Act may include civil, but not criminal, penalties.

The DOJ reminds market participants that it:

> also often uses other laws to fight illegal activities, including laws that prohibit false statements to Federal agencies, perjury, obstruction of justice, conspiracies to defraud the United States, and mail and wire fraud. Each of these crimes carries its own fines and imprisonment terms which may be added to the fines and imprisonment terms for antitrust law violations.[12]

Additionally, the Clayton Act[13] is another civil statute that allows for (1) mergers or acquisitions that are likely to lessen competition to be blocked and (2) state lawyers general or private parties to bring civil suits for damages.

Most states have enacted antitrust laws that function similarly to the federal laws.[14] State lawyers general may seek to enforce these laws, which apply to conduct occurring within their state. For example, in 2009 the Texas lawyer general filed an antitrust lawsuit against Memorial Hermann Healthcare System alleging it had unreasonably restrained trade in violation of the Texas Business and Commerce Code.[15] Specifically, Memorial Hermann was accused of taking steps to discourage health insurers from contracting with a local competing hospital. The complaint noted that Houston was the relevant geographic area and that the Texas lawyer general brought the action "as *parens patriae* on behalf of the citizens of the State of Texas, and in his capacity as the designated enforcer of the Constitution and the statutes of the State of Texas."[16] Memorial Hermann ultimately agreed to an injunction and paid the state $700,000.

The Application of the Sherman Act: Evolutions of the "Per Se" Rule, "Rule of Reason" Test, "Inherently Suspect" Test, and Financial Integration

While the Sherman Act's language prohibits "every contract . . . in restraint of trade or commerce," the Supreme Court has long held that such a literal interpretation is not what Congress intended.[17] The Court therefore established the "rule of reason" test whereby, under the particular circumstances, an agreement that is found to amount to an *unreasonable* restraint on competition is prohibited.[18] The rule of reason was summarized as follows by the Court:

> The true test of legality is whether the restraint imposed is such as merely regulates and perhaps thereby promotes competition or whether it is such as may suppress or even destroy competition. To determine that question the court must ordinarily consider the facts peculiar to the business to which the restraint is applied; its condition before and after the restraint was imposed; the nature of the restraint and its effect, actual or probable. The history of the restraint, the evil believed to exist, the reason for adopting the particular remedy, the purpose or end sought to be attained, are all relevant facts. This is not because a good intention will save an otherwise objectionable regulation or the reverse; but because knowledge of intent may help the court to interpret facts and to predict consequences.[19]

However, the Court has held certain arrangements as so egregious on their face as to not justify a full rule of reason analysis. In describing this "per se illegal" rule, the Court stated:

> There are certain agreements or practices which because of their pernicious effect on competition and lack of any redeeming virtue are conclusively presumed to be unreasonable and therefore illegal without elaborate inquiry as to the precise harm they have caused or the business excuse for their use. This principle of *per se* unreasonableness not only makes the type of restraints which are proscribed by the Sherman Act more certain to the benefit of everyone concerned, but it also avoids the necessity for an incredibly complicated and prolonged economic investigation into the entire history of the industry involved, as well as related industries, in an effort to determine at large whether a particular restraint has been unreasonable—an inquiry so often wholly fruitless when undertaken. Among the practices which the courts have heretofore deemed to be unlawful in and of themselves

are price fixing . . . division of markets . . . group boycotts . . . and tying arrangements . . . .[20]

Physician joint ventures in which prices may be fixed across a provider network would naturally raise antitrust questions. To this end, in the seminal *Arizona v. Maricopa County Medical Society* case, the Supreme Court found an agreement among competing physicians to establish maximum fees for payment from participants in specific insurance plans to be per se illegal. However, the Court also noted that partnerships among physicians, including price-fixing, where they share financial risk, may be proper. Specifically, the Court noted these agreements must be " . . . analogous to partnerships or other joint arrangements in which persons who would otherwise be competitors pool their capital and share the risks of loss as well as the opportunities for profit."[21] Accordingly, the Agencies now generally afford rule of reason treatment to physician joint ventures where there is *substantial financial integration* among the participants whereby the perceived benefits to consumers outweigh anticompetitive concerns.

Therefore, to determine whether an arrangement's effect on competition is "unreasonable," courts typically apply the per se illegal and rule of reason tests.

Per Se Illegal

In the health care context, agreements that always or almost always raise prices or reduce output with no meaningful integration of firms' activities or pro-competitive effect from agreement are per se illegal.[22] Plaintiffs are not required to prove the agreement had an actual anticompetitive effective, and defendants are not permitted to introduce evidence of an agreement's pro-competitive effect.

Rule of Reason

Under the rule of reason, the defendant is permitted to show the pro-competitive benefits of an agreement. The plaintiff must prove the anticompetitive effects of the arrangement and that the pro-competitive benefits could be obtained using less-restrictive measures.[23]

Inherently Suspect

The FTC has also advanced an "inherently suspect" analysis, which was described in *North Texas Specialty Physicians v. FTC*[24] as being a close cousin to the per se illegal test, or a "quick look" version rule of reason analysis. In that case, the court finding that a physician group participated in horizontal price-fixing without any pro-competitive efficiencies noted:

> The Supreme Court has recognized, however, that even when practices are not condemned by a *per se* rule, a fullblown rule-of-reason analysis is not always required. An "abbreviated or 'quick-look' analysis under the rule of reason" is appropriate when an "observer with even a rudimentary understanding of economics could conclude that the arrangements in question would have an anticompetitive effect on customers and markets." Stated another way, "quick-look analysis carries the day when the great likelihood of anticompetitive effects can easily be ascertained." The "inherently suspect" paradigm that the FTC employed in the present case is a "quick-look" rule-of-reason analysis.[25]

In the inherently-suspect approach, there is a presumption of anticompetitive harm based on the nature of the agreement. However, the defendant may offer evidence of the pro-competitive benefits of the agreement.[26]

Ancillary Restraints Doctrine

Health care joint ventures may result in contractual arrangements that place restraints on certain forms of competition. The Supreme Court has held that the rule of reason is "the standard for testing the enforceability of covenants of restraint of trade which are ancillary to a legitimate transaction."[27] Later, Judge Robert Bork elaborated on this premise by stating:

> To be ancillary, and hence exempt from the *per se* rule, an agreement eliminating competition must be subordinate and collateral to a separate, legitimate transaction. The ancillary restraint is subordinate and collateral in the sense that it serves to make the main transaction more effective in accomplishing its purpose.[28]

An lawyer in the DOJ's Antitrust Division summarized the Agencies' general view of ancillary restraints in the joint venture context, which should be taken into consideration with exclusivity and similar agreements:

> The ancillary restraints doctrine holds that a restraint collateral to a legitimate joint venture, limiting the ability of participants to compete outside the venture, is assessed as part of a package that includes the formation of the venture, if at the time the restraint was adopted, the restraint had an organic connection to [the] venture and was reasonably necessary to make the venture more efficient or effective in achieving its procompetitive purposes.[29]

The FTC has issued advisory opinions to health care joint ventures analyzing whether the competitive restraints are outweighed by their necessity and pro-competitive nature of the arrangement.[30] As discussed later in this chapter, there are also circumstances for ACOs when the Agencies will presume ancillarity.

Federal Agency Health Care Antitrust Guidance before the Affordable Care Act

Joint Statements of Antitrust Enforcement Policy in Health Care

The Agencies have issued a series of statements of antitrust enforcement policy in health care to address uncertainty around how they approach antitrust enforcement regarding mergers and joint venture activities in the health care sector. In September 1993, the Agencies' first such release included six policy statements related to (1) hospital mergers, (2) hospital joint venture involving high-technology or other expensive medical equipment, (3) physicians' provision of information to purchasers of health care services, (4) hospital participation in exchanges of price and cost information, (5) health care providers' joint purchasing arrangements, and (6) physician network joint ventures. In light of the comments the Agencies received, in September 1994 they issued a second joint statement, which superseded the prior year's release, and added new statements relating to hospital joint ventures involving specialized clinical services, providers' collective provision of fee-related information to purchasers of health care services, and analytical principles relating to various multiprovider networks. In August 1996, the Agencies released their third and most recent set of statements ("1996 Statements").[31] The 1996 Statements revised the guidance related to physician joint ventures and other multiprovider networks, as described further below, while leaving the other statements unchanged.

Statement of the Department of Justice and the Federal Trade Commission Enforcement Policy on Physician Network Joint Ventures ("Statement 8")

Statement 8 describes how the Agencies view specific conduct by physician networks and whether it falls under an antitrust safety zone, will be afforded rule of reason treatment, or is considered per se illegal.

Safety Zones under Statement 8

The Agencies outline the types of arrangements that are unlikely to raise substantial competitive concerns, and therefore are unlikely to be challenged by the Agencies, absent extraordinary circumstances. The safety-zone criteria are dependent on a number of factors, such as whether the physician network is "exclusive" or "nonexclusive." Exclusive ventures restrict the physician participants from contracting or affiliating with other networks. Nonexclusive ventures do not impose these restrictions, so physician participants are able to affiliate with other networks.

Exclusive Physician Network Safety Zone	Nonexclusive Physician Network Safety Zone
Physician participants share substantial financial risk in providing all the services that are jointly priced through the network and constitute *20 percent or less* of the physicians in each physician specialty with active hospital staff privileges who practice in the relevant geographic market. In markets with fewer than *five physicians* in a particular specialty, an exclusive physician network joint venture otherwise qualifying for the antitrust safety zone may include one physician from that specialty, *on a nonexclusive basis*, even though the inclusion of that physician results in the venture consisting of more than 20 percent of the physicians in that specialty.	Physician participants share substantial financial risk in providing all the services that are jointly priced through the network and constitute *30 percent or less* of the physicians in each physician specialty with active hospital staff privileges who practice in the relevant geographic market. In markets with fewer than *four physicians* in a particular specialty, a nonexclusive physician network joint venture otherwise qualifying for the antitrust safety zone may include one physician from that specialty, even though the inclusion of that physician results in the venture consisting of more than 30 percent of the physicians in that specialty.

Rule of Reason under Statement 8

Physician networks that do not fall under one of the antitrust safety zones can still be afforded rule of reason treatment if the joint venture is reasonably necessary to accomplish its pro-competitive benefits, such as significant efficiencies that benefit consumers. For example, when physicians have agreed to share substantial financial risk and are incentivized to meet overall efficiency goals for the joint venture. This may include capitation, global fee arrangements, fee withholds, and cost- or utilization-based bonuses or penalties.[32] Importantly, Statement 8 introduces the notion of *clinical integration* as an avenue, other than sharing substantial financial risk, for affording rule of reason treatment. Statement 8 provides examples of clinical integration, including establishing goals relating to quality and utilization, evaluating individual participant and overall network performance in meeting those goals, and modifying practices when necessary based on those evaluations.[33]

Per Se Illegal under Statement 8

Arrangements purporting to have pro-competitive benefits, but in reality impede competitive forces will be "treated as unlawful conspiracies or cartels, whose price agreements are *per se* illegal."[34] Situations that suggest an arrangement may be anticompetitive and be considered *per se* illegal include:

- statements evidencing anticompetitive purpose;
- recent history of anticompetitive behavior or collusion, including efforts to obstruct or undermine the development of managed care;
- anticompetitive structure of the network, such as a very high percentage of local area physicians without any efficiency justification;
- absence of any factors with the potential to increase efficiency and/or competition;
- anticompetitive collateral agreements; and
- absence of measures to mitigate the network from having anticompetitive effects outside of the network.[35]

Statement of the Department of Justice and the Federal Trade Commission Enforcement Policy on Multiprovider Networks ("Statement 9")

Statement 8 dealt with networks composed solely of physicians, which are one type of multiprovider network. All other multiprovider networks, such as physician-hospital organizations, networks with physicians and nonphysicians, etc., are addressed in Statement 9. The analyses are similar relating to rule of reason treatment and per se illegal arrangements, but there are some distinctions to be aware of. For example, Statement 9 concludes that "[b]ecause multiprovider networks involve a large variety of structures and relationships among many different types of health care providers, and new arrangements are continually developing, the Agencies are unable to establish a meaningful safety zone for these entities."[36] Additionally, the rule of reason analysis under Statement 9 considers the effects of horizontal agreements (between competitors) and vertical agreements (among noncompetitors that inhibit competition in another market). It should be noted that vertical price restraints had been considered per se illegal by the Supreme Court for almost a century.[37] However, the Court reversed itself in 2007, finding that "vertical price restraints are to be judged by the rule of reason."[38]

Antitrust Guidelines for Collaborations among Competitors

In April 2000, the Agencies issued the above titled guidance outlining their analytical approach to evaluating competitor joint ventures.[39] The intent was to allow businesses to better understand potential antitrust implications and therefore promote pro-competitive collaborations while discouraging harmful anticompetitive arrangements. While the guide notes that it is consistent with the framework established in the 1996 Statements, it is not industry specific. However, this release provides further guidance on how the Agencies approach their per se and rule of reason analyses, which practitioners should find insightful.

Improving Health Care: A Dose of Competition

After conducting extensive hearings, workshops, and independent research, the Agencies issued *Improving Health Care: A Dose of Healthy Competition* in June 2004.[40] This policy document addresses two main questions: (1) What is the role of competition in health care, and how can it be improved to benefit consumers? (2) How has, and how should, antitrust enforcement be conducted to protect competition in health care? The voluminous report examines competition within several health care groups including physicians, hospitals, third-party payment programs, insurers, and pharmaceuticals. Chapter 2 of the report provides background information and specific guidance on how the Agencies analyze provider network joint ventures (independent practice associations (IPAs) and physician-hospital organizations (PHOs)), financial integration (sharing financial risk), and clinical integration (improving the quality of care that member physicians provide).

To supplement the guidance provided in Statement 8, this 2004 policy statement lays out a list of questions the Agencies are likely to ask when reviewing a physician network justifying its joint venture based upon clinical integration:

1. What do the physicians plan to do together from a clinical standpoint?
    - What specific activities will (and should) be undertaken?
    - How does this differ from what each physician already does individually?

- What ends are these collective activities designed to achieve?

2. How do the physicians expect to actually accomplish these goals?
   - What infrastructure and investment is needed?
   - What specific mechanisms will be put in place to make the program work?
   - What specific measures will there be to determine whether the program is in fact working?
3. What basis is there to think that the individual physicians will actually attempt to accomplish these goals?
   - How are individual incentives being changed and realigned?
   - What specific mechanisms will be used to change and realign the individual incentives?
4. What results can reasonably be expected from undertaking these goals?
   - Is there any evidence to support these expectations, in terms of empirical support from the literature or actual experience?
   - To what extent is the potential for success related to the group's size and range of specialties?
5. How does joint contracting with payors contribute to accomplishing the program's clinical goals?
   - Is joint pricing reasonably necessary to accomplish the goals?
   - In what ways?
6. To accomplish the group's goals, is it necessary (or desirable) for physicians to affiliate exclusively with one IPA, or can they effectively participate in multiple entities and continue to contract outside the group?

- Why or why not?[41]

Clinical Integration in Health Care: A Check-Up

On May 29, 2008, the FTC sponsored a workshop for industry participants to discuss clinical integration developments among health care providers. The public comments and materials from participants, including representatives from the FTC, commercial insurance carriers, hospital and physicians associations, and law firms are available for review on the FTC's website.[42] For example, the FTC staff presenter listed "the guiding principles we follow," including how the FTC "does not pick winners and losers."[43]

Federal Agency Antitrust Guidance on ACOs after the Affordable Care Act

Following the enactment of the Affordable Care Act on March 23, 2010, a number of federal antitrust and health care agencies held workshops or issued proposed guidance regarding ACOs participating in the Medicare Shared Savings Program (SSP):

- On October 5, 2010, the FTC, Health and Human Services Office of the Inspector General and the Centers for Medicare and Medicaid Services (CMS) held the Workshop regarding ACOs and Implications regarding Antitrust, Physician Self-Referral, Anti-kickback and Civil Monetary Penalty Laws.[44] The participating agencies discussed how safe harbors for ACOs might be structured and an expedited antitrust review process for ACOs falling outside of those safe harbors.
- On March 31, 2011, the Agencies jointly issued the Proposed Statement of Antitrust Enforcement Policy Regarding Accountable Care Organizations Participating in the Medicare Shared Savings Program ("Proposed ACO Statement").[45] The two primary differences between the Proposed ACO Statement and the final policy statement are (1) the proposed policy would have applied only to collaborations formed after March 23, 2010, where the final policy (except for the voluntary agency review) applies to all collaborations, and (2) the proposed policy would have imposed a mandatory agency antitrust review where the final policy provides for a voluntary review.
- On May 9, 2011, the FTC hosted a workshop[46] with industry participants seeking input on the Proposed ACO Statement. As previously noted, one of the major critiques of the proposed policy was the requirement for a mandatory review as opposed to a voluntary review, which the Agencies later acquiesced to.

DOJ and FTC Statement of Antitrust Enforcement Policy Regarding Accountable Care Organizations Participating in the Medicare Shared Savings Program ("ACO Statement")

After receiving feedback on the Proposed ACO Statement, the Agencies released their final ACO policy statement.[47] The ACO Statement (1) provides an antitrust safety zone for certain ACOs, (2) affords rule of reason treatment for ACOs meeting the requirements, (3) describes specific conduct by ACOs that may raise anticompetitive concerns, and (4) provides a voluntary expedited 90-day agency review for newly formed ACOs seeking antitrust guidance.

Safety Zone under the ACO Statement

The ACO Statement establishes a safety zone for ACOs that is not likely to raise competitive concerns. Absent extraordinary circumstances (such as collusion or exchanging of price information),[48] the Agencies will not challenge an ACO that meets the safety-zone requirements. Each of the ACO participants providing the same service[49] must have a combined share of 30 percent or less of each common service in each participant's primary services area (PSA), where two or more ACO participants provide that service to patients from that PSA. The PSA for each participant is constructed using the lowest number of postal zip codes from which the ACO participant draws at least 75 percent of its patients, calculated separately for all physician, inpatient, and outpatient services. Whether a participant is exclusive or nonexclusive (allowed to contract with private payers through other entities) to the ACO is also taken into consideration. However, to qualify for the safety zone, hospitals and ambulatory surgical centers must be nonexclusive.

Under the rural exception, the safety zone also permits an ACO to exceed the 30 percent PSA share by including one physician or physician practice group per specialty from each designated rural area on a nonexclusive basis. Similarly, a rural hospital may be included even if it would cause an ACO participant's PSA share to exceed 30 percent.

The dominant provider limitation applies to an ACO that includes a participant with a greater than 50 percent share of any service in its PSA that no other ACO participant provides to patients in that PSA. In such cases, to remain in the safety zone, (1) the ACO participant must be non-exclusive to the ACO, and (2) the ACO cannot require a private payer to contract exclusively with the ACO or otherwise inhibit them from dealing with other ACOs or provider networks.

Rule of Reason under the ACO Statement

Similar to the 1996 Statements, the Agencies note that an ACO falling outside of the safety zone can still be structured to be pro-competitive and therefore not raise antitrust concerns. If an ACO meets the CMS eligibility requirements for and participates in the SSP, and uses the same governance and leadership structures and clinical and administrative processes for both Medicare and commercial markets, then the Agencies will apply the rule of reason treatment. Accordingly, the Agencies will treat joint negotiations with private payers as reasonably necessary to an ACO's primary purpose of improving health care delivery.[50]

Concurrent with the release of the ACO Statement, CMS released the requirements for ACOs participating in the SSP, which include promoting evidence-based medicine and patient engagement, reporting on quality and cost metrics to monitor provider performance, and coordinating care among primary care physicians and specialists.[51] Participating ACOs will need to be in compliance with these and other requirements in the CMS rules.

Ancillarity under the ACO Statement

The Proposed ACO Statement suggested that the Agencies may infer ancillarity, stating that:

> if a CMS-approved ACO provides the same or essentially the same services in the commercial market, the Agencies have determined that the integration criteria are sufficiently rigorous that joint negotiations with private-sector payers will be treated as subordinate and reasonably related to the ACO's primary purpose of improving health care services.[52]

The final ACO Statement included similar language, although it did not specifically carry over the "subordinate" language. However, FTC staff has recently confirmed that "the Agencies will presume or assume ancillarity and then give rule of reason treatment for the ACO"[53] meeting the rule of reason analysis requirements described above.

Conduct for ACOs to Avoid

The ACO Statement outlines specific conduct that may raise antitrust concerns. These include the improper sharing of competitively sensitive information (e.g., pricing for services outside of the ACO), and for ACOs with high PSA share or other indicia of market power:

1. preventing or discouraging private payers from directing or incentivizing patients to choose certain providers, including providers that do not participate in the ACO, through "anti-steering," "anti-tiering," "guaranteed inclusion," "most-favored-nation," or similar contractual clauses or provisions;
2. tying sales (either explicitly or implicitly through pricing policies) of the ACO's services to the private payer's purchase of other services from providers outside the ACO (and vice versa), including providers affiliated with an ACO participant (e.g., an ACO should not require a purchaser to contract with all of the hospitals under common ownership with a hospital that participates in the ACO);
3. contracting on an exclusive basis with ACO physicians, hospitals, ambulatory surgery centers, or other providers, thereby preventing or discouraging those providers from contracting with private payers outside the ACO, either individually or through other ACOs or analogous collaborations; and
4. restricting a private payer's ability to make available to its health plan enrollees cost, quality, efficiency, and performance information to aid enrollees in evaluating and selecting providers in the health plan, if that information is similar to the cost, quality, efficiency, and performance measures used in the SSP.[54]

Voluntary Agency Antitrust Review

ACOs that intend to participate in the commercial market and SSP and, as of March 23, 2010, had not yet signed or jointly negotiated contracts with private payers or participated in the SSP may request expedited antitrust guidance from the Agencies.[55] The instructions and request cover sheet are available on the FTC's website. The request must be submitted to both the DOJ and FTC by mail or electronically. The FTC/DOJ ACO working group described the process:

> Within 90 days of receiving all of the documents and information described in the ACO Policy Statement, the reviewing Agency will advise the ACO that the ACO's formation and operation, as described in the documents and information provided to the Agency, does not likely raise competitive concerns (or does not likely raise competitive concerns conditioned on an understanding that the ACO will take certain steps to remedy specific concerns), potentially raises competitive concerns, or likely raises competitive concerns. As is current practice, both the request letter and the reviewing Agency's response will be made public consistent with applicable Agency confidentiality provisions.[56]

Short of the formal voluntary review process, the Agencies also encourage market participants to informally call their staff to discuss their particular situation.

As shown in the table below, the market(s) an ACO participates in will determine which agency guidance is most applicable.

ACOs Exclusive to the Medicare Program	ACOs Exclusive to the Commercial Market	ACOs That Operate in Both Medicare and Commercial Market
An FTC Health Care Division staff lawyer stated succinctly, "If an ACO is operating only as part of the Medicare program, generally antitrust is not an issue because the government is setting the prices paid to the providers." This was evidenced when, in March 2012, a proposed ACO requested a voluntary review. The applicant was advised that it was not eligible for the review process since it did not intend to operate in any commercial market, and after an offer of informal guidance from the antitrust agency, it was subsequently approved to participate in the SSP.	As its name suggests, the ACO Statement is not applicable to ACOs that do not participate in the SSP. The level of financial and/or clinical integration of these entities would be analyzed under the previously issued Statement 8 or 9 of the 1996 Statements. The Agencies may analyze the extent of financial and/or clinical integration, market power, ancillarity of any restrictive agreements, and perceived benefits to consumers.	The ACO Statement is applicable and provides the most up-to-date guidance on how to structure joint ventures operating in these markets without raising anticompetitive concerns. "The ACO policy statement provides more lenient treatment of ACOs operating on the commercial side when that ACO also participates in the Medicare program."

FTC Advisory Opinions Related to Health Care Joint Ventures

In addition to the Agencies' statements on enforcement policy, the FTC staff has issued a number of advisory opinions to market participants seeking an analysis under the rule of reason that a proposed health care joint venture would not be deemed per se illegal and that the staff would therefore not recommend enforcement action. These advisory opinions are insightful particularly in the absence of any voluntary expedited reviews under the ACO Statement. The FTC staff issued favorable opinions regarding proposed joint ventures in the following matters:

- MedSouth, Inc. (February 19, 2002[57] and June 18, 2007[58])
- Greater Rochester Independent Practice Association, Inc. (September 17, 2007)[59]

- TriState Health Partners, Inc. (April 13, 2009)[60]
- Norman Physician Hospital Organization (February 13, 2013)[61]

However, in the Suburban Health Organization, Inc., advisory opinion, the FTC staff did not find the level of integration and potential benefits to consumers outweighed the restraints on competition, stating:

> We believe that SHO's program involves some integration among its hospital participants that has the potential to generate efficiencies in the provision of physician services, but also that the integration and potential efficiency benefits appear to be significantly limited. Further, the program's competitive restraints do not appear to be reasonably necessary in order to achieve its potential efficiencies, and therefore would unnecessarily eliminate competition. Accordingly, we believe that the program's restraints would not be permissible under the antitrust laws.[62]

Developments since the ACO Statement

In April 2013, the FTC and DOJ ACO working group issued a summary of activities since the issuance of the ACO Statement through March 31, 2013.[63] The ACO working group reported that the Agencies had received 33 questions, mostly related to PSA share or voluntary review, and have made the responses available on their websites.[64] The ACO working group also reported that the Agencies had only received two requests for voluntary expedited 90-day reviews. One request was moot since the proposed ACO was only participating in the SSP and therefore was ineligible for the review, and the other request was withdrawn by the applicant prior to the commencement of the review. Therefore, market participants do not yet have the benefit of substantive responses from the Agencies to requests for voluntary reviews of ACOs.

Conclusion

The Agencies have hosted numerous workshops and issued several policy statements and advisory opinions on health care joint ventures. The Agencies, aided with claims data from CMS, will be monitoring participating ACOs for potential antitrust violations. The fact that market participants have not availed themselves of voluntary expedited reviews of ACOs may suggest there is sufficient clarity around the level of financial and/or clinical integration required to receive positive rule of reason treatment and the types of conduct to avoid being challenged as per se illegal or inherently suspect. From the antitrust and consumer perspectives, time will tell whether these collaborations are truly pro-competitive.

Notes

1. *Remarks of FTC Chairman Jon Leibowitz as Prepared for Delivery FTC/CMS Workshop on Accountable Care Organizations*, FED. TRADE COMM'N (Oct. 5, 2010), http://www.ftc.gov/sites/default/files/documents/public_statements/remarks-ftc-chairman-jon-leibowitz-prepared-delivery-ftc/cms-workshop-accountable-care-organizations/101005acoremarks.pdf.

2. *About the FTC*, FED. TRADE COMM'N, http://www.ftc.gov/ftc/about.shtm (last visited Mar. 18, 2014).

3. FED. TRADE COMM'N, OVERVIEW OF FTC ANTITRUST ACTIONS IN HEALTH CARE SERVICES AND PRODUCTS 1 (Mar. 2013), *available at* http://www.ftc.gov/sites/default/files/attachments/competition-policy-guidance/hcupdate.pdf.

4. *About the Division*, DEP'T OF JUSTICE, http://www.justice.gov/atr/about/index.html (last visited Mar. 18, 2014).

5. *Guide to the Antitrust Laws: The Enforcers*, FED. TRADE COMM'N, http://www.ftc.gov/bc/antitrust/enforcers.shtm (last visited Mar. 18, 2014).

6. *See* FED. TRADE COMM'N & DEP'T OF JUSTICE, IMPROVING HEALTH CARE: A DOSE OF COMPETITION ch. 2, § IV, at 33–34 (July 2004) [hereinafter 2004 DOSE OF COMPETITION], *available at* http://www.ftc.gov/sites/default/files/documents/reports/improving-health-care-dose-competition-report-federal-trade-commission-and-department-justice/040723healthcarerpt.pdf.

7. 15 U.S.C. §§ 1–7.

8. 15 U.S.C. § 1.

9. 15 U.S.C. §§ 41–58.

10. 15 U.S.C. § 45(a).

11. *See* Holloway v. Bristol-Myers Corp., 485 F.2d 986 (D.C. Cir. 1973); Carlson v. Coca-Cola Co., 483 F.2d 279 (9th Cir. 1973).

12. *Antitrust Enforcement and the Consumer*, DEP'T OF JUSTICE, http://www.justice.gov/atr/public/div_stats/antitrust-enfor-consumer.pdf (last visited Mar. 18, 2014).

13. 15 U.S.C. §§ 12–27.

14. *See, e.g.*, N.Y. GEN. BUS. LAW §§ 340–347 (the Donnelly Act).

15. Complaint, State v. Mem. Hermann Healthcare Sys. (Tex. Harris Cnty. Jan. 26, 2009), *available at* www.oag.state.tx.us/newspubs/releases/2009/012609hermann_pop.pdf.

16. *Id.*

17. United States v. Joint Traffic Ass'n, 171 U.S. 505 (1898).

18. Standard Oil Co. v. United States, 221 U.S. 1, 88 (1911).

19. Chi. Bd. of Trade v. United States, 246 U.S. 231, 238 (1918).

20. N. Pac. Ry. Co. v. United States, 356 U.S. 1, 5 (1958).

21. Arizona v. Maricopa Cnty. Med. Soc'y, 457 U.S. 332, 356 (1982).

22. Presentation Materials from Healthcare Antitrust Fundamentals, American Bar Association, Health Law Section, Antitrust Law Section, Center for Professional Development and Young Lawyers Division (Mar. 7, 2013).

23. *Id.*

24. 528 F.3d 346 (5th Cir. 2008).

25. *Id.* at 360–61.

26. Polygram Holding, Inc. v. FTC, 416 F.3d 29, 36 (D.C. Cir. 2005).

27. Nat'l Soc'y of Prof'l Eng'rs v. United States, 435 U.S. 679, 689 (1978).

28. Rothery Storage & Van Co. v. Atlas Van Lines, Inc., 792 F.2d 210, 224 (D.C. Cir. 1986).

29. Gregory J. Werden, Sr. Econ. Counsel, Antitrust Div., The Ancillary Restraints Doctrine: Rule of Reason v. Per Se: Where Are the Boundaries Now?, Program at the American Bar Association Section of Antitrust Law Meeting (Mar. 29–31, 2006), *available at* http://apps.americanbar.org/antitrust/at-committees/at-s1/pdf/spring-materials/2006/werden06.pdf.

30. *See* Letter from Markus H. Meier, Asst. Dir., Bureau of Competition, Health Care Div., to Christi Braun & John Miles, Regarding Greater Rochester Independent Practice Association, Inc., Advisory Opinion (Sept. 17, 2007), *available at* http://www.ftc.gov/sites/default/files/documents/advisory-opinions/greater-rochester-independent-practice-association-inc./gripa.pdf; Letter from Meier to Braun, Regarding TriState Health Partners, Inc., Staff Advisory Opinion (Apr. 13, 2009), *available at* http://www.ftc.gov/sites/default/files/documents/advisory-opinions/tristate-health-partners-inc./090413tristateaoletter.pdf.

31. DEP'T OF JUSTICE & FED. TRADE COMM'N, STATEMENTS OF ANTITRUST ENFORCEMENT POLICY IN HEALTH CARE (Aug. 1996) [hereinafter 1996 STATEMENTS], *available at* http://www.justice.gov/atr/public/guidelines/1791.pdf.

32. 2004 DOSE OF COMPETITION, *supra* note 6, ch. 2, § IV, at 35.

33. 1996 STATEMENTS, *supra* note 31, at 83.

34. *Id.* at 74.

35. *Id.*

36. *Id.* at 107.

37. Miles Med. Co. v. John D. Park & Sons Co., 220 U.S. 373 (1911).

38. Leegin Creative Leather Prods. v. PSKS, Inc., 551 U.S. 877, 882 (2007).

39. FED. TRADE COMM'N & DEP'T OF JUSTICE, ANTITRUST GUIDELINES FOR COLLABORATIONS AMONG COMPETITORS (Apr. 2000), *available at* http://www.ftc.gov/os/2000/04/ftcdojguidelines.pdf.

40. 2004 DOSE OF COMPETITION, *supra* note 6.

41. *Id.* ch. 2, § IV, at 40–41.

42. *Clinical Integration in Health Care: A Check-Up*, FED. TRADE COMM'N (May 29, 2008), http://www.ftc.gov/news-events/events-calendar/2008/05/clinical-integration-health-care-check.

43. Markus Meier, Fed. Trade Comm'n, Presentation on Clinical Integration: "A Patient History" (May 29, 2008), *available at* http://www.ftc.gov/sites/default/files/documents/public_events/clinical-integration-health-care-check/meier-presentation-clinical-integration-workshop.pdf.

44. *Available at* http://www.ftc.gov/opp/workshops/aco/index.shtml#webcast.

45. Statement of Antitrust Enforcement Policy Regarding Accountable Care Organizations Participating in the Medicare Shared Savings Program, 76 Fed. Reg. 21,894–902 (proposed Apr. 19, 2011) [hereinafter Proposed ACO Statement].

46. Fed. Trade Comm'n, Workshop, Another Dose of Competition: Accountable Organizations and Antitrust (May 9, 2011), *available at* http://www.ftc.gov/opp/workshops/aco2/index.shtml.

47. Statement of Antitrust Enforcement Policy Regarding Accountable Care Organizations Participating in the Medicare Shared Savings Program, 76 Fed. Reg. 67,026–32 (Oct. 28, 2011) [hereinafter ACO Statement].

48. *Id.* at 67,028.

49. The ACO Statement defines a service as a primary specialty for physicians, Major Diagnostic Categories (MDC) for inpatient facilities, and outpatient categories as defined by CMS for outpatient facilities.

50. ACO Statement, *supra* note 47, at 67,028.

51. Medicare Shared Savings Program: Accountable Care Organizations, 76 Fed. Reg. 67,976–77 (Nov. 2, 2011).

52. Proposed ACO Statement, *supra* note 45, at 21,896.

53. Alpa G. Davis, Staff Attorney, Fed. Trade Comm'n, Health Care Div., Statement at American Bar Association Healthcare Antitrust Fundamentals Seminar (Mar. 7, 2013) (preceded by the standard introductory disclaimer that her comments did not necessarily reflect the views of the commission or any commissioner).

54. ACO Statement, *supra* note 47, at 67,030.

55. DOJ/FTC *Frequently Asked Questions about Voluntary Expedited Review under the Statement of Antitrust Enforcement Policy Regarding ACOs Participating in the Medicare Shared Savings Program*, *available at* http://www.justice.gov/atr/public/health_care/276478.pdf.

56. FTC/DOJ *ACO Working Group Questions and Answers Relating to Voluntary Review under the ACO Policy Statement* (last updated Mar. 31, 2013) [hereinafter *ACO Working Group Q&A*], *available at* www.justice.gov/atr/public/health_care/295587.pdf.

57. Letter from Jeffrey Brennan, Asst. Dir., Fed. Trade Comm'n, to John Miles, Regarding MedSouth, Inc., Staff Advisory Opinion (Feb. 19, 2002), *available at* http://www.ftc.gov/bc/adops/medsouth.shtm.

58. Letter from Markus Meier, Asst. Dir., Bureau of Competition, Health Care Div., Regarding Follow-Up to MedSouth, Inc., Staff Advisory Opinion (June 18, 2007), *available at* http://www.ftc.gov/sites/default/files/documents/advisory-opinions/medsouth-inc./070618medsouth.pdf.

59. Letter from Meier to Braun & Miles, *supra* note 30.

60. Letter from Meier to Braun, *supra* note 30.

61. Letter from Markus Meier, Asst. Dir., Bureau of Competition, Health Care Div., to Michael Joseph, Regarding Norman Physician Hospital Organization Advisory Opinion (Feb. 13, 2013), *available at* http://www.ftc.gov/sites/default/files/documents/advisory-opinions/norman-physician-hospital-organization/130213normanphoadvltr_0.pdf.

62. Letter from David Pender, Acting Asst. Dir., Bureau of Competition, Health Care Servs. & Prods. Div., to Clifton Johnson & William Thompson, Regarding Suburban Health Organization, Inc. (Mar. 28, 2006), *available at* http://www.ftc.gov/sites/default/files/documents/advisory-opinions/suburban-health-organization/suburbanhealthorganizationstaffadvisoryopinion03282006.pdf.

63. *ACO Working Group Summary of Activities*, *supra* note 58.

64. *ACO Working Group Q&A*, *supra* note 56.

6

ACOs and the Impact on Bundle Payments and Value-Based Purchasing

"[The Affordable Care Act's] payment reform provisions, including value-based purchasing, accountable care organizations (ACOs), bundled payments, and the medical home, target improvements in quality and efficiency at a time when health care costs comprise 23 percent of the federal budget."

—Deloitte Center for Health Solutions.[1]

Overview

On November 2, 2011, the U.S. Department of Health and Human Services (HHS) published the final rule implementing section 3022 of the Affordable Care Act (ACA).[2] Section 3022 addresses Medicare payments to providers participating in Accountable Care Organizations (ACOs). ACOs have the ability to not only collect traditional fee-for-service payments under Medicare Part A and Part B, but also can take advantage of "provisions designed to improve the quality of Medicare services, support innovation and the establishment of new payment models, better align Medicare payments with provider costs, strengthen program integrity within Medicare, and put Medicare on a firmer financial footing."[3]

As part of these initiatives, the Secretary of HHS was required to establish the Medicare Shared Savings Program.[4] The primary purpose behind Medicare Shared Savings Program (SSP) was to establish ACOs. The Shared Savings Program also had a "three part aim" of delivery system reform efforts of ACA. These core components are (1) better care for individuals, (2) better health for populations, and (3) lower growth in Medicare Parts A and B expenditures.[5] The payment-reform provisions present in ACA include ACOs, value-based purchasing, and bundled payments.[6] Two concepts designed to assist in transforming the current fee-for-service system to a quality and efficiency model are value-based purchasing and bundle payments. Therefore, the focus of this chapter is to explain value-based purchasing, highlight how bundle payments augment the current fee-for-service system, and illustrate what this means for ACO participants.

Value-Based Purchasing

The premise behind value-based purchasing is to connect payment directly to the quality of care provided. As part of the Medicare Shared Savings Program, the Centers for Medicare and Medicaid Services (CMS) established hospital value-based purchasing as required under ACA and applies to Medicare's inpatient prospective payment system (IPPS). According to CMS, hospital value-based purchasing holds providers accountable for the provision of health care services based on cost and quality and rewards the quality of care delivered via transparency and payment incentives.[7]

Value-based purchasing is a program that evolved over the past decade, even though it became viable through the passage of ACA in 2010. Three laws had a significant impact on its current implementation: the Medicare Modernization Act of 2003, the Deficit Reduction Act of 2005, and the Medicare Improvements for Patients and Providers Act of 2008.[8] The Medicare Modernization Act commissioned the Institute of Medicine to "identify and prioritize options to align performance to payment in Medicare." Building on the Medicare Modernization Act, the Deficit Reduction Act of 2005, section 5001(b), required HHS to build upon the Reporting Hospital Quality Data for Annual Payment Update and develop a plan to implement value-based purchasing. Finally, Medicare Improvements for Patients and Providers Act of 2008, section 131(d), required HHS to develop a value-based purchasing transition plan for providers.[9]

Value-based purchasing can best be described as such: "Hospitals serving Medicare beneficiaries will be eligible to receive incentive payments in 2013 for patients with high-volume conditions (i.e., chronic heart failure, acute MI, pneumonia, surgeries, and health care-associated infections)."[10] Subsequent care settings, such as ambulatory surgery centers, physician reimbursement, and long-term care hospitals, will also become incorporated into this initiative. Notably, participation is mandatory for all hospitals, except those limited exceptions, treating Medicare beneficiaries.[11]

Staying on top of the quality measures is critical because of the emphasis on the total value-based purchasing score. The score is not only composed of quality measures for high-volume conditions, but 30 percent of the total score is based on patient experience score. In turn, a score that is below the financial qualification threshold (53 versus 70) potentially disqualifies hospitals from receiving millions of dollars in financial incentives.[12] As entities such as Geisinger, Integrated Health Association, and Prometheus Payment demonstrate, there are different types of incentives that are being used to implement value-based purchasing and related initiatives such as bundled payments.[13]

Bundled Payments

The bundled payments initiative was established by CMS under ACA. Specifically, section 1115A of the Social Security Act (as added by section 3021 of ACA) authorized CMS to create the Innovation Center to evaluate "innovative payment and service delivery models to reduce program expenditures . . . while preserving or enhancing the quality of care" for persons participating in Medicare, Medicaid, or the Children's Health Insurance Program.

With the passage of ACA, Congress authorized the Secretary of HHS of various models on a pilot-program basis. Like the Recovery Audit Contractor Program, which was created under the Medicare Modernization

Act of 2003, began as a pilot program in part of the United States, and expanded nationwide in January 2010 under section 302 of the Tax Relief and Healthcare Reform Act of 2006, the Innovation Center has the ability to try different programs in parts of the country before expanding the program nationwide. With the focus on connecting payments for the gamut of services Medicare beneficiaries obtain during "an episode of care," the bundled payments initiative includes four models of care.[14] A discussion of the various models, as well as the one most suited to ACOs, follows.

The Ability of ACOs to Capitalize on Bundled Payments and Value-Based Purchasing

Intended to encourage the development of ACOs in Medicare, section 3022 required the Secretary of HHS to establish the Medicare Shared Savings Program.[15] As part of this program, various programs designed to base incentive payments on the quality of care delivered are required. ACOs are a conduit for implementing bundled payments and value-based purchasing.[16] The models are broken down as follows[17]:

- *Model 1*—Retrospective Acute Care Hospital Stay Only—applies to inpatient stays in an acute-care hospital setting. With the exception of certain circumstances, Medicare will pay the hospital a discounted rate and continue to pay physicians separately under the Medicare physician fee schedule. Participation commenced around January 2014 and includes most Medicare-fee-for-service discharges.
- *Model 2*—Retrospective Acute Care Hospital Plus Post-Acute Care—applies to 48 different clinical condition episodes and includes the inpatient stay, as well as the post-discharge period of 30, 60, or 90 days.
- *Model 3*—Retrospective Post-Acute Care Only—commences when post-acute care services with participating facilities (i.e., skilled-nursing facility, inpatient rehabilitation facility, long-term care hospital, or home health agency). These services must begin within 30 days of discharge from the acute-care hospital and end at either 30, 60, or 90 days. This

is based on 48 different clinical episodes that are captured in the corresponding diagnosis-related grouping code.

- *Model 4*—Acute-Care Hospital Stay Only—CMS pays a single, prospectively determined amount to the acute-care hospital for all services rendered during the episode of care by the hospital, physicians, and other practitioners. While the hospital receives remuneration, physicians and other practitioners submit "no-pay" claims to Medicare and are remunerated by the hospital out of the bundled payment. Significantly, related readmissions for 30 days after the discharge are included in the bundled payment amount. Hospital-acquired conditions can adversely impact the overall reimbursement.[18]

Of the four types of models, Model 4 seems well suited to ACOs, which allow for coordination of care and performance based on quality and outcomes. As the chart below illustrates, ACOs can take different forms.[19]

ACO Entity	Structure/ Governance	Programs	Payment Model with Payer	Physician Compensation Model
Accountable Care Alliance (Omaha, NE)	Limited liability organization created by two hospital systems and three physician groups.	Commercial.	Initially only shared savings.	Three potential models: (1) full employment; (2) contracts with performance standards; or (3) independent physicians with common protocols.
Arizona Connected Care (Tucson, AZ)	Limited liability company—physician-led partnership with TMC Healthcare System.	Medicare SSP, commercial, and Medicaid SSP.	Shared savings with expectation to adopt downside risk later.	75 percent of savings shared with primary care physician, specialists and hospital based on patient volume and quality of care.

ACO Entity	Structure/ Governance	Programs	Payment Model with Payer	Physician Compensation Model
Cheyenne ACO (Cheyenne, WY)	Limited liability company—50-50 partnership between physician group and CRMC.	Delaying Medicare SSP application for one year.	Medicare risk models under consideration.	To be determined.
MACIPA Pioneer ACO (Cambridge, MA)	No joint legal structure—independent practice associations and hospital negotiate payer contracts jointly.	Medicare Advantage, commercial plans, Medicare Pioneer.	Upside and downside risk arrangements.	Physicians receive fee for service.

An ACO may also structure itself as a "hybrid deal"—that is, "an innovative type of joint venture between for-profit and not-for-profit entities designed for the purpose of improving health care delivery in a mutually accretive manner."[20] This may enable increased benefits of capitalizing on various economies of scale, coordination of patient care, and value-based purchasing and bundled-payment initiatives. Importantly, entities should look at state law, tax law, antitrust law, and anti-kickback law, in addition to the impact on accounting.

Overall, Model 4 may provide the most streamlined opportunities in back-office management, coordination of care, and optimizing the added benefits of ACOs. It is crucial to bear in mind the goals for CMS's value-based purchasing initiatives. Some of the goals include improved clinical quality; identifying areas of underuse, overuse, and misuse of services; and reduction of adverse events.[21] ACOs, as part of the Medicare Supplemental Security Income (SSI), offer a structure to capitalize on improved quality of care, increased efficiencies across the revenue cycle, and additional payments.

Conclusion

ACOs enable the participants to capitalize on complementary shared savings programs that focus on quality and outcomes. In addition to the financial payments available from Medicare, ACOs may be able to streamline back-office functions, reduce the incidence of hospital-acquired conditions by aligning incentives, and mitigating exposure to relevant laws. Overall, bundled payments and value-based purchasing offer ACOs additional options when implementing these programs.

Notes

1. *Issue Brief: Value-Based Purchasing: A Strategic Overview for Health Care Industry Stakeholders*, Deloitte Ctr. for Health Solutions (2011), http://www.deloitte.com/assets/Dcom-UnitedStates/Local%20Assets/Documents/Health%20Reform%20Issues%20Briefs/US_CHS_ValueBasedPurchasing_031811.pdf.

2. 76 Fed. Reg. 67,802 (Nov. 2, 2011); Patient Protection and Affordable Care Act, Pub. L. No. 111-148 (Mar. 23, 2010); Health Care and Education Reconciliation Act of 2010, Pub. L. No. 111-152 (Mar. 30, 2010) (amending certain provisions of Public Law 111-148 collectively form the Affordable Care Act).

3. 76 Fed. Reg. 67,802, 67,803 (Nov. 2, 2011).

4. Pub. L. No. 111-148, § 3022.

5. 76 Fed. Reg. 67,802.

6. *Issue Brief: Value-Based Purchasing: A Strategic Overview for Health Care Industry Stakeholders*, *supra* note 1, at 1.

7. Medicare Hospital Value-Based Purchasing Plan Development (U.S. Dep't of Health & Human Servs., Issue Paper, 1st Public Listening Sess., Jan. 17, 2007), *available at* https://www.cms.gov/AcuteInpatientPPS/downloads/hospital_VBP_plan_issues_paper.pdf; *Roadmap for Implementing Value Driven Health Care in the Traditional Medicare Fee-for-Service Program*, Ctrs. for Medicare & Medicaid Servs., https://www.cms.gov/QualityInitiativesFenInfo/downloads/VBPRoadmap_OEA_1–16_508.pdf (last visited Mar. 18, 2014).

8. Inst. of Med., Rewarding Provider Performance: Aligning Incentives in Medicare (Pathways to Quality Health Care Series 2007), *available at* http://www.nap.edu/catalog/11723.html; *Roadmap for Implementing Value Driven Health Care in the Traditional Medicare Fee-for-Service Program*, *supra* note 7; ; Development of a Plan to Transition to a Medicare Value-Based Purchasing Program for

Physician and Other Professional Services (U.S. Dep't of Health & Human Servs., Issue Paper, Dec. 9, 2008).

9. *Ibid.*

10. *Issue Brief: Value-Based Purchasing: A Strategic Overview for Health Care Industry Stakeholders*, *supra* note 1, at 6.

11. *See* http://www.hfma.org/Templates/InteriorMaster.aspx?id=23002; http://www.hfma.org/Templates/InteriorMaster.aspx?id=2054.

12. http://www.hfma.org/Templates/Print.aspx?id=22975.

13. *Issue Brief: Value-Based Purchasing: A Strategic Overview for Health Care Industry Stakeholders*, *supra* note 1, at 8.

14. *Bundled Payments of Care Improvement (BPCI) Initiative: General Information*, CTRS. FOR MEDICARE & MEDICAID SERVS., http://innovation.cms.gov/initiatives/bundled-payments/# (last visited Mar. 18, 2014).

15. 76 Fed. Reg. 67,802, 67,803 (Nov. 2, 2011).

16. *Id.* at 67,880. "Medical errors are a major source of morbidity and mortality in the United States, and patient safety initiatives that reduce the number of these events are a critical focus for CMS and the Department. However, we recognize that not all ACOs will have participating hospitals, but, for those ACOs that do have hospitals, we do not believe this approach is duplicative of hospital value-based purchasing program efforts, which calculate such measures at a hospital patient population level and not at an ACO assigned beneficiary population level. We also recognize that some HACs may be reduced but not eliminated, as one commenter noted. Reporting remains an important issue for effectively tracking health care acquired conditions."

17. *Supra* note 8.

18. As part of the Deficit Reduction Act (DRA) of 2005, specifically section 5001(c), which required the Secretary of HHS to identify conditions that (a) are high cost or high volume or both, (b) result in the assignment of a case to a diagnosis-related grouping that has a higher payment when present as a secondary diagnosis, and (c) could reasonably have been prevented through the application of evidence-based guidelines. If certain conditions were not initially documented as present on admission, then hospitals will not receive additional payment for treating these identified conditions. *See Hospital-Acquired Conditions (Present on Admission Indicator)*, CTRS. FOR MEDICARE & MEDICAID SERVS., http://www.cms.gov/Medicare/Medicare-Fee-for-Service-Payment/HospitalAcqCond/index.html?redirect=

/HospitalAcqCond/06_Hospital-Acquired_Conditions.asp (last updated Feb. 10, 2014); Fact Sheet, *Medicare Learning Network: Hospital-Acquired Conditions (HAC) in Acute Inpatient Prospective Payment System (IPPS) Hospitals* (Dep't of Health & Human Servs. & Ctrs. for Medicare & Medicaid Servs., ICN No. 901045, Oct. 2012) (relaying that in August 2012, CMS published the Inpatient Prospective Payment System (IPPS) Fiscal Year (FY) 2013 Final Rule; examples of HACs include catheter associated urinary tract infections, vascular catheter-associated infection, and surgical site infection following select orthopedic procedures).

19. This table also appears in Chapter 2 in relation to respondeat superior.

20. Bryan Cali & Casey Quinn, *A New Tool for System Building: Hybrid Deals Are Enabling Unlikely Partners to Come Together in Developing Strategies for Care Delivery and Population Management*, Healthcare Fin. Mgmt. Mag., May 2013, at 72.

21. *Issue Brief: Value-Based Purchasing: A Strategic Overview for Health Care Industry Stakeholders*, *supra* note 1, at 4.

7 How to Communicate Effectively with Physicians

Introduction and Cultural Comparisons

Chapter 7 is written with the lawyer or consultant in mind. This author's experience with the formation of physician-owned Accountable Care Organizations (ACOs) has underscored the need for every lawyer to understand the physician as client. The author's 10 years of medical practice and 15 years of law practice have culminated in this chapter, which is intended to provide the nonphysician reader with some practical insight on physicians and how to communicate effectively with them. In addition, this chapter will strive to deliver information that most people could not learn from a book or from interviewing the average businessman or lawyer.

Perhaps the best starting point would be to compare and contrast the cultural differences in training between a doctor and a lawyer, and how the culture that evolves from the two professions are such worlds apart that, when put in the context of a "real world" situation—such as a business deal or the negotiation of the formation of an Accountable Care Organization—the worlds may collide and reach an insurmountable impasse that may interrupt negotiations or may kill a deal.

Below are some broad cultural comparisons about the two professions:

Medicine

1. There is a clearly defined social hierarchy among peers and subordinates.
2. The most senior physician has the "gospel" answer on treatment.
3. The diagnosis or conclusion is derived from an analysis of the data or facts.

Law

1. There is a social "equalizer" among peers.
2. The new lawyer is more familiar with the new laws and has the "latest answer" to a given legal problem.
3. The lawyer begins the analysis with the desired outcome or conclusion, then finds the facts necessary to support that conclusion.

The "culture" created in both the medical and legal professions are greatly influenced by the vendors that cater to them during their "formative years" in training. For example, it was historically not uncommon for medical students, residents, and practicing physicians to receive "freebies" from pharmaceutical companies. The influence of the freebies became so pronounced that in 2002 the Pharmaceutical Research and Manufacturers of America (PhRMA) issued a set of guidelines for its member companies to follow when it comes to the relationship between drug reps and doctors. The voluntary code significantly changed how drug-company representatives interact with doctors. Changes range from restricting gifts to limiting consulting contracts offered to doctors.

PhRMA was inspired to come up with the code after years of criticism from groups such as Families USA and Public Citizen. PhRMA already had a set of guidelines on this topic, but its board decided that one of the best ways to thwart the criticism and prevent any appearance of impropriety was to come up with a stricter code.

After PhRMA enacted its guidelines, the Office of Inspector General for the U.S. Department of Health and Human Services issued guidelines similar to PhRMA's code, except with more severe penalties. Companies that fail to follow the department's rules could face a federal investigation that could lead to civil penalties.

Similarly, it is not uncommon for law students and young lawyers to receive "perks" and other promotional items from legal search engine companies. They can take the form of social event sponsorships, free thumb drives (USB drives), free online access, etc. Therefore, if one is trying to negotiate effectively with either professional, one should take care not to get lumped into the same category as the "drug reps" or "legal research reps," or else the expectations may be more than one can afford.

Educational Background

Doctors may have as much as 20,000 to 30,000 or more hours of training under their belts after medical school, and not even one-quarter of 1 percent of that training is devoted to business, finance, or law. When doctors go out in the "real world" to run their own small business or medical practice, they typically turn only to each other to get business, financial, or legal advice. Truly a case of the blind leading the blind.

Below is a breakdown on the doctor's education:

College	4 years
Medical School	4 years
Internship	1 to 2 years
Residency	3 to 7 years
Fellowship	1 to 2 years
Grand Total:	13 to 19 years of education after high school

Financial Realities

Typically, the 13 to 19 years of education after high school translates into 13 to 19 years of financial debt.

In 2012, the Association of American Medical Colleges reported that the average educational debt of graduates of the class of 2012 was

$166,750. At least 79 percent of those indebted graduates have a debt of at least $100,000; 62 percent of indebted graduates have a debt of at least $150,000; and at least 86 percent of graduating medical students carry outstanding loans.

Imagine starting your professional career with $150,000 of debt. How do doctors do it? Remember, you are dealing with individuals who have historically had relatively easy access to student loans and credit throughout their training. When you factor in the amount of time the resident physician in training spends in the hospital in some residency programs, the average pay works out to about $1.25 per hour. Many physicians have pushed their "delayed gratification button" to its limits by the time they have completed their residency training. Therefore, it is not uncommon to see them overspending on their first home or car or boat, etc.

Many physicians finish their medical specialty training, then venture off to start up and operate a complex small business called a medical practice—all without any training in business, finance, or law. Perhaps the real economic reason why doctors can survive making bad investments or bad spending decisions is because they have cash flow.

It is very important to have an understanding of the cash-flow patterns of the physician's specialty because it can greatly influence the physician's ability to purchase or invest in any products. Clearly, specific medical specialties will have unique "sale cycles" of revenue. Sometimes the revenue is impacted by the paying habits of a third-party payer (or insurance company). Other times, the revenue is influenced by the demographics of the immediate surroundings of the doctor's office, or the revenue may be impacted by the time of the year (e.g., winter, or cold and flu season).

For example, private-practice obstetrician-gynecologist (ob-gyn) doctors do not realize any significant income pay per patient until nine months after the patient is initially seen: Once the baby is delivered, the ob-gyn is paid on average $2,000 per delivery.

Another example is the emergency room (ER) physician. Depending on the demographics of the county in which a hospital emergency room is located, an ER doctor may provide as much as 46 percent to 62 percent of indigent care (i.e., to patients that cannot or will not pay for the services). Many non-surgeons often increase their revenue stream by simply seeing more patients or by performing more complex or well-reimbursed procedures.

Generally, surgeons will have undergone more technical training than non-surgeons. Although, some nonsurgical specialties may have subspecialties that equal or surpass the amount of time spent in surgical training programs. Although the list below is by no means comprehensive, it is intended to give the reader a general overview of some of the medical specialties one is likely to come across.

Surgeons

- general surgeons
- ob-gyn
- orthopedists
- ophthalmologists
- otolaryngologists
- plastic surgeons
- cardiothoracic surgeons
- neurosurgeons

Invasive Non-Surgeons

- invasive cardiologists
- invasive radiologists
- gastroenterologists
- dermatologists
- pathologists

Non-Surgeons

- family practitioners
- pediatricians
- geriatric physicians
- internal medicine physicians
- cardiologists
- radiologists

Indeed, it is critically important to have some understanding of the medical specialty of your prospective doctor client before making that first visit. Try to get an understanding of what traits are demanded by the physician's medical specialty, and that will give the best clue as to what kind of business interaction can be anticipated. From a general perspective, it is instructive to distinguish between the surgeons and non-surgeons.

Surgeons

What kind of demeanor would be needed if a job required split-second decisions based upon limited information, and someone's life depended on those decisions?

- strong-willed
- little or no self-doubt, even if wrong
- ready to act quickly even with limited information, regardless of potential consequences
- not ready or willing to take advice or rely on others to make decisions or perform the act, even if others may be more qualified or experienced

In a business meeting or negotiation, this translates into potentially a meeting with

- a "difficult" person;
- someone resistant to taking professional advice;
- someone not likely to appreciate (or pay for) your services;
- someone not ready or willing to rely on you to make any major decisions for them;
- someone not readily willing to commit to a project; or
- someone ready to commit to a project, even if they have little to no understanding of the complete ramifications of that decision.

Non-Surgeons

What kind of demeanor would be needed if a job required listening daily to many people talk about their physical and emotional problems and having to make multiple life-altering decisions based upon information overload regarding possible side effects of those decisions?

- good listener
- ready to commit only after considering all the benefits and consequences
- "paralysis by analysis"
- very risk-averse

The specialty of internal medicine requires a different demeanor than that of the general surgeon. Internal medicine specialists tend to be more introspective and slower to act. From a business perspective, this usually translates into a long sales cycle.

In a business meeting or negotiation, this translates into potentially a meeting with

- a client that is paralyzed from making any business decisions;
- someone resistant to acting upon professional advice;
- someone who may take an extremely long time to commit to a project;
- someone who may be intimidated with *not enough* information available in a field unfamiliar to them; or
- someone who may be willing to proceed with a project but without the financial or educational resources to start the project.

If someone is about to meet with an internal medicine physician, it is a good idea for that person to have all the reference materials ready to back up the verbal representations. Both parties will likely want to read all your written materials before committing to anything. Please note that there are always exceptions to the stereotypes between surgeons and non-surgeons, but it certainly gives an advantage over competitors if lawyers understand what is in the prospective client's head.

Physician Groups

If working with a group of physicians, lawyers will likely encounter one or two individuals that will tend to have more dominant roles in the group. These are the physicians that lawyers must focus their attention on because these are the individuals that will influence greatly the decisions made by others in the group. I refer to these individuals as the "alpha doctors." Although the alpha doctors will have significant impact upon the overall decision making in the group, whoever has the ability to influence the "committee collective mentality" prevails. Interestingly, many physicians in groups often blindly follow each other, particularly when making business decisions.

Most physicians are compensated on a fee-for-service basis. Therefore, many will have difficulty understanding the concept of hourly billing. In fact, if lawyers send physicians an invoice that they are not anticipating, the lawyers may lose not only their business but also business from the physicians' colleagues as well. In addition, it is sometimes best to estimate how much time will be spent on a project, then charge a flat fee for the service. It will more often lead to a more pleasant business experience with doctors.

The best time to meet with physicians is early in the morning or very late in day (i.e., evening). In addition, physicians will expect you to respond quickly to a call—just as the doctor himself or herself would respond to an urgent call from a hospital or clinic. In fact, this author's personal experience has shown that some of the most productive meetings he has had with doctors began at 5:00 a.m. or at 7:00 p.m.—the times before doctors start seeing patients or after they have finished seeing patients for the day.

Word travels fast among physicians or physician groups. Make sure to try to make each client experience a pleasant one.

Even if it is not possible to answer physicians' questions right away or answer their phone calls in person, it is best to have an assistant or secretary return the call promptly and then schedule some type of appointment to get back to physicians. If lawyers do not return the calls promptly, it is likely physicians will perceive they are not very good at what they do.

Real World Application: The Physician-Owned ACO

Picture a room filled with about 50 to 70 physicians—both primary care doctors and surgical specialists. In this author's first ACO, such was the case as the nuances of the ACO were explained and the process of structuring an appropriate corporate entity to meet the needs of the ACO was described.

Within minutes, the surgical specialists piped up, asserting their dominance in the group. Many of the specialists were asking questions geared toward the acquisition of more shares in the corporate entity than their fellow primary care brethren. Most of the primary care physicians just sat quietly, trying to process the information and trying to determine if there was some way they could gain some "equal footing" with the specialists. In many health care physician investments, surgical specialists have historically dominated the investment landscape—whereas most primary care physicians stood at the sidelines trying to find ways they may be able to participate on a level playing field with the specialists.

The ACO provides the level playing field, and even turns the tables—as the Centers for Medicare and Medicaid Services (CMS) assigns the Medicare beneficiaries to the provider that has seen that patient most often. For example, let's say that we have two physicians that submit patient lists of 2,000 names apiece. One physician is a primary care doctor and the other physician is a cardiothoracic surgeon. In our example, if both physicians turn their lists and tax identification numbers to CMS, the primary care doctor will probably receive credit for at least 1,800 covered lives from that list of 2,000, whereas the cardiothoracic surgeon will likely receive credit for only 140.

Important to note is the fact that some specialists (e.g., endocrinologists, nephrologists, oncologists, etc.) actually see their patients more frequently than those patients see their primary care physician. In these instances, that specialist will get the "credit" for the assigned beneficiary.

For anyone interested in forming a physician-owned ACO, it is perhaps best to invite only primary care doctors (or even specialists that see their patients more frequently than the primary care physicians) to the initial organization meeting of the ACO. It is these individuals that will receive the most "credit" for the Medicare beneficiaries and will facilitate more efficiently the path to reaching the threshold of 5,000 Medicare beneficiaries in order to become recognized as an ACO. The choice of entity and specific corporate structuring of the ACO will be addressed in Chapter 8.

Bottom line: It is essential for any lawyer working with physicians to have an innate understanding of their physician client—as that may make the difference between a good and a bad client experience.

8 Determining a Corporate Structure for the ACO

Deciding upon the best corporate structure for an Accountable Care Organization (ACO) is perhaps the most critical initial decision to be made after making the decision to form an ACO. The Affordable Care Act (ACA) does not provide specific requirements as to the choice of legal entity for an ACO, but first and foremost, governance and structure should be the central focus—and the degree of cooperation and cohesiveness among the physicians within the ACO will impact significantly the structure that one chooses. An ACO may be owned primarily by a health care system/entity or primarily by physicians (i.e., a physician-owned ACO, or POACO). This author's experience is based primarily upon POACOs, and this chapter will therefore focus upon the intricacies of choosing the appropriate corporate structure for the POACO.

By definition, an ACO is a formally organized legal entity, composed of physicians, hospitals, and/or other relevant health-service professionals that have chosen to work together and are responsible through contractual agreements with payers for providing a broad set of health care services to their Medicare patients. ACOs are designed to reward providers that are able to manage chronic disease and meet certain quality measures, including such measures as reducing hospital admissions and emergency room visits. If the quality of care improves and costs are constrained, the systems can share in the savings. This legal entity is accountable for organizing and aligning health care services in order to deliver seamless and coordinated care—whether the ACO is a single corporate structure or an organized network of independent but associated health care professionals.

ACOs will take different forms depending upon local market conditions and levels of existing competition among providers. Unless an ACO is able to reduce the fragmentation of care, waste, and variability, it will not experience any long-term success. Currently, the Medicare Shared Savings Program (SSP) described in section 3022 of the ACA provides the most guidance on design of the ACO, and the Centers for Medicare and Medicaid Services (CMS) has also proposed specific rules of conduct for the SSP. It is important to note that the SSP is a Medicare program, but the structure of the ACO should be designed to accommodate both governmental as well as nongovernmental (e.g., commercial insurance) payers.

The ACO legal entity may be structured as a corporation, partnership, limited liability company, foundation, or other entity permitted under applicable federal, state, or tribal law.[1] The entity must be authorized to conduct business in each state in which it operates for the purposes outlined above.[2] An existing legal entity that is eligible to be an ACO is permitted to continue its use of this structure if it meets the other ACO eligibility and governance requirements.[3]

Indeed, CMS attests that "if an existing legal entity adds ACO participants that will remain independent legal entities (such as through a joint venture among hospitals or group practices), it would have to create a new legal entity to do so."[4] These comments indicate that an ACO formed by two or more independent ACO participants (such as a hospital and physician group practice) must be established as a new legal entity separate from the other ACO participants with its own TIN.[5]

Shared savings payments will be made directly to the entity designated as the ACO, regardless of whether that entity is enrolled in the Medicare program.[6] While the final rule does not dictate the manner an ACO distributes shared savings among its participants, CMS finalizes the requirement that an ACO must describe in its ACO application its plan for using and distributing shared savings in furtherance of the goals of the SSP.[7]

An ACO must have a separate and unique governing body (i.e., board of directors, board of managers, etc.), particularly in cases when the ACO "comprises multiple, otherwise independent ACO participants."[8] If the organization designated as the ACO is an existing entity, then the ACO governing body "may be the same as the governing body of that existing entity, provided that it satisfies the other requirements" for shared governance, leadership, and management.[9]

The ACA does not require an ACO governing body to provide proportionate representation by ACO participants, representation by all ACO participants, or inclusion of any specific categories of providers, suppliers, or stakeholders.[10] CMS, however, allows ACOs flexibility in determining the governing body's composition, provided that ACO participants are given the opportunity for "meaningful participation" in the ACO's governance.[11]

The governing body must have a transparent governing process with a conflict-of-interest policy and broad responsibility for oversight of the ACO, the governing body's clinical and administrative processes, and its strategic direction in furtherance of the goals of the SSP.[12] In addition, the members of the governing body must have a fiduciary duty to the ACO and act in accordance with that duty.[13]

To ensure that ACOs are "provider driven," the final rule requires that at least 75 percent of the ACO's governing body be composed of ACO participants.[14] This allows for up to 25 percent participation by non-providers such as health-plan, management-company, and community stakeholders.[15] CMS requires that the ACO governing body include one Medicare beneficiary representative who does not have a conflict of interest.[16]

CMS declines to dictate how voting control is apportioned by an ACO.[17] The final rule permits ACO governing body members to "serve in a similar or complementary manner for an ACO participant."[18]

In a change from the proposed rule, the final rule permits some flexibility as to compliance with the governance rules. More specifically, in cases in which the composition of the ACO's governing body does not meet the governance requirement, the regulations state that an ACO can describe the differences and how "the ACO will involve ACO participants in innovative ways in ACO governance or provide meaningful representation in ACO governance by Medicare beneficiaries."[19] The final rule requires that "[t]he ACO governing body must have a conflict of interest policy that applies to members of its governing body."[20]

ACOs must have a leadership and management structure that "includes clinical and administrative systems that align with and support the goals of the SSP."[21] CMS also requires management of the ACO's operations by an officer, executive, general partner, or manager capable of influencing or directing clinical practice so as to improve efficiency, processes, and outcomes and whose appointment and removal are controlled by the ACO's governing body.[22]

The clinical oversight must be managed by a medical director at a senior level who is a physician and one of the ACO's providers/suppliers and who meets certain other requirements set forth in the regulations;[23] however, this position is not required to be full time as originally proposed.[24] In addition, an ACO must have a quality-assurance and improvement program with oversight by a "qualified health care professional," who is not required to be a physician.[25]

ACO participants and providers/suppliers must demonstrate a "meaningful commitment" to the ACO's mission.[26] In the commentary, CMS states that this "meaningful commitment" can be in the form of human capital (such as service on the governing board or committees or participating in operations), financial investment (e.g., by contributing capital for infrastructure needs), or a commitment to comply with and implement the ACO's required processes and performance standards.[27]

CMS shall consider innovative ACOs with alternate management structures that do not meet the regulatory requirements.[28] This flexibility is similar to that provided in connection with the composition of the governing body.[29] The comments indicate that the intent is to provide greater flexibility on ACO governance and management structures where there are other considerations potentially impacting the structure.[30] Documentation of the management and leadership structures is required as part of the ACO application process.[31]

The general eligibility, legal, and governance requirements under the final rule are somewhat more flexible than those under the proposed rule. The eligibility provisions are broader than under the proposed rule, permitting more types of entities to participate as ACOs. CMS expanded the eligibility rules to include entities organized under federal or tribal laws, as well as federally qualified health centers and rural health centers. In addition, the final rule permits CMS to give consideration to an organization with an innovative management or governance structure that does not meet the regulatory requirements for operating as an ACO for purposes of the SSP.

An ACO must become "accountable for the quality, cost, and overall care of the Medicare fee-for-service beneficiaries assigned to the ACO" in order to participate in the SSP.[32] In addition, an ACO may participate in the one-sided model without taking on any downside risk.[33] ACOs that operate under the two-sided model and meet or exceed a minimum loss ratio must still share losses with Medicare.[34]

Under 42 C.F.R. § 425.20 of subpart E, the Medicare fee-for-service beneficiary will be assigned to an ACO by CMS. CMS will employ a "preliminary" prospective assignment methodology with final retrospective reconciliation. Beneficiaries will be assigned to an ACO in a preliminary manner at the beginning of the performance year based on the most recent data available, and assignment will be updated quarterly based on the most recent 12 months of data. Final assignment then will be determined after the end of each performance year based on data from the performance year.

CMS also indicates that assignment is limited for purposes of determining the population of Medicare fee-for-service beneficiaries for whose care the ACO is accountable under subpart F (Quality and Other Reporting Requirements) and whether an ACO has achieved savings under subpart G (Shared Savings and Losses). Assignment to an ACO therefore in no way diminishes or restricts a beneficiary's rights to exercise free choice in determining where to receive health care services.

Finally, for purposes of assigning beneficiaries, primary care services are identified by selected health care common procedure coding system codes (HCPCS) and G codes as indicated in the definition of primary care services under 42 C.F.R. § 425.20.[35] The agency also clarifies that beneficiaries who are assigned to an ACO will not have diminished or restricted rights to exercise free choice in determining where to receive health care services.

The basic assignment methodology used by CMS is described in 42 C.F.R. § 425.402. Essentially, the system is designed to balance maintaining a strong emphasis on primary care while ultimately allowing for assignment of beneficiaries on the basis of how they actually receive their primary care services. Under this approach, assignment to an ACO first is based on the receipt of primary care services from primary care physicians (defined as a physician with a primary specialty designation of general practice, family practice, internal medicine, or geriatric medicine). Those beneficiaries who have not received primary care services from primary care physicians then may be assigned to an ACO on the basis of primary care services provided by other physicians and practitioners.

To assign Medicare fee-for-service beneficiaries to a particular ACO, CMS will begin by identifying all patients that had at least one primary care service from a physician who is an ACO provider or supplier.

CMS employs the following stepwise methodology for determining assignment:

In the first step, CMS will identify all primary care services rendered by primary care physicians during either (1) the most recent 12 months (for purposes of preliminary prospective assignment and quarterly updates to the preliminary prospective assignment) or (2) the performance year (for purposes of final assignment). The beneficiary is assigned to an ACO if the allowed charges for primary care services furnished to the beneficiary by all the primary care physicians who are ACO providers or suppliers, are greater than the allowed charges for primary care services furnished by primary care physicians who are (1) providers or suppliers in any other ACO and (2) not affiliated with any ACO and identified by a Medicare-enrolled tax identification number (TIN).

In the second step, CMS will consider the remainder of the beneficiaries who have received at least one primary care service from an ACO physician but who have not received a primary care service from any primary care physician, either inside or outside the ACO. The beneficiary will be assigned to an ACO if the allowed charges for primary care services furnished to the beneficiary by all ACO professionals (e.g., specialists, nurse-practitioners, physician assistants, clinical nurse specialists) who are ACO providers or suppliers in the ACO are greater than the allowed charges for primary care services furnished by (1) all ACO professionals who are ACO providers or suppliers in any other ACO and (2) other physicians, nurse-practitioners, physician assistants, and clinical nurse specialists who are unaffiliated with an ACO and are identified by a Medicare-enrolled TIN.

An ACO is required to have at least 5,000 beneficiaries assigned to it annually.[36] If at any time during the performance year an ACO's assigned population falls below this number, the ACO will be "issued a warning and placed on a CAP [Corrective Action Plan]."[37] The CAP could include a provision to add more primary care providers to the ACO or other changes needed to increase the number of assigned beneficiaries. While under the CAP, the ACO remains eligible for shared savings and losses during the performance year for which the warning and CAP were issued.[38] If the ACO's assigned population does not go back up to at least 5,000 or more by the end of the next performance year, the ACO's agreement will be terminated and the ACO will not be eligible to share in savings for that performance year.[39]

The basis for assignment of beneficiaries to an ACO is where they receive a "plurality of their primary care services."[40] However, CMS made significant changes to the fundamental assignment method. Responding to strong criticism of the retrospective method originally proposed, CMS established a prospective assignment method coupled with a reconciliation process to be performed annually.[41] CMS indicates in the comments that an ACO "will not receive an assignment of those beneficiaries that choose not to receive care from ACO providers."[42]

Similarly, beneficiaries who choose to receive care from particular providers within an ACO may be assigned to that ACO "regardless of whether they are 'unmanageable' or noncompliant with treatment."[43] CMS emphasized in the comments that "avoidance of such beneficiaries . . . will result in termination of an ACO's participation agreement."[44] CMS also finalized the requirement that an ACO executive with authority to bind the ACO must certify that the ACO's participants are "willing to become accountable for, and to report to us on, the quality, cost, and overall care" of the beneficiaries assigned to that ACO.[45]

As a result, the parties eligible to form ACOs have been expanded in the final rule from the five categories originally proposed to seven categories, as follows:

1. ACO professionals in group practice arrangements
2. networks of individual practices of ACO professionals

3. partnerships or joint venture arrangements between hospitals and ACO professionals;
4. hospitals employing ACO professionals
5. Critical Access Hospitals that bill Medicare for facility and other professional services;
6. rural health centers; and
7. federally qualified health centers[46]

An ACO professional is a physician or a practitioner as provided in the Social Security Act, and a "hospital" is defined as an acute care hospital reimbursed under the hospital inpatient prospective payment system.[47] Other Medicare-enrolled entities that are not identified above are eligible to participate in the SSP through an ACO formed by one or more of the eligible formation entities enumerated.[48]

ACOs differ from managed care and capitation models in that the focus of much of the metrics is upon quality of care and outcomes data. If an ACO receives a global payment for the care of a specific patient population, that payment is generally a capitated payment. The ACO health care providers focus upon the utilization and quality of health care services provided. There is also a risk adjustment that occurs, which takes into consideration the level of illness of a patient population and presumably deters health care providers from avoiding the sicker and more burdensome patients.

When one starts up a POACO, it will yet be unproven whether or not the entity will generate sufficient shared savings to make a profit. As we have seen in the experience of the Pioneer ACOs, not all of them were able to generate a profit from shared savings: Only 18 out of 32 Pioneer ACOs were able to generate substantial savings after the first year of the program. Meanwhile, 12 ACOs did not achieve significant savings, and two owe Medicare an estimated $4 million. Seven ACOs left the program in favor of the SSP. Perhaps the most common complaint among the ACOs that encountered difficulties with the Pioneer ACO Model was that CMS had not adequately addressed cost-saving measures that predated the program.

At the time of this writing, there are estimates of almost 500 ACOs in the United States, with over 200 being commercial ACOs and the rest being sponsored by either Medicare or Medicaid. The experiences of the

Pioneer ACO program demonstrated a correlation between the size of the sponsoring health system as well as the magnitude of operating costs and the success of the Pioneer ACO.

Consequently, a POACO venture should be treated like any entrepreneurial health care venture. The POACO entity must have at least 75 percent ownership/control by physicians. Non-physicians may own and/or control no more than 25 percent of the entity. The 25 percent portion opens the door to private equity or at least a potential capital partner that is not also a provider. This capital partner will be crucial in facilitating the information technology (IT) infrastructure necessary to provide the analysis and metrics for outcomes data needed for reimbursement.

An ACO must be constituted as a legal entity for purposes of receiving and distributing shared savings, repaying shared losses, and complying with all SSP requirements, including governance requirements and quality performance standards.[49] In this author's experience, at least 60 percent of an ACO should be composed of primary care physicians so that one is most likely to achieve the requisite 5,000 covered lives. Whenever the formation of an ACO is contemplated in a particular Medicare region, typically only the primary care physicians in the area are invited to estimate whether or not we will likely have the threshold number of covered lives. In our experience, it takes approximately 50 to 60 physicians—with 60 percent being primary care—in order to reach that requisite number.

In an ideal setting, the ACO will receive a global payment for services rendered to the defined patient population served by the ACO. Payment and incentives within the ACO are structured to promote a shared sense of responsibility for both cost and quality. An optimal payment structure should take into consideration the components of fee-for-service, a care management fee, and a pay-for-performance component.

The entity should be structured such that there is no confusion about who is responsible for the company's obligations. If a corporation, partnership, or limited liability company (LLC) is formed, capitalized, and operated properly, the new legal entity constitutes a separate and distinct "person" in the eyes of the law. The ACO entity, rather than any individual physician or group that formed it, will be liable for the debts and obligations of the ACO. While this is not true in all situations (e.g., where the owner has personally guaranteed a debt of the company or where the owners have failed to provide appropriate capitalization), the "limited liability" that a separate legal entity provides can and often does prove to be crucial.

Basically, four types of legal entities are available, all formed under the laws of the state in which the entity is formed: (1) the regular corporation (or subchapter C corporation), (2) the subchapter S corporation, (3) the partnership, and (4) the limited liability company. No single entity type is the right choice for all ACOs, but each should be considered and juxtaposed against the mission and initiatives of the physicians within the ACO in order to arrive at the best entity type for the group.

Below is a brief summary of the legal entities most typically used, as well as an articulation of some of the advantages and disadvantages of each.

Subchapter C Corporations

The subchapter C corporation (a C corporation) was traditionally the preferred choice of legal entity for most businesses. In many states where a professional entity is required for a physician practice, these would take the form of a professional corporation, or PC. Because of its long tradition and the many years of court cases that have clarified the legal relationships that flow from the C corporation, it remains a popular choice for many entrepreneurial health care ventures. Most larger companies, and virtually all publicly traded companies, are C corporations. The principal disadvantage is the burden of "double taxation" that falls on a C corporation and its shareholders.

C corporations have the advantage of providing solid limited liability protection, subject to few limitations regarding management of the business. In addition, C corporations afford health care entrepreneurs significant flexibility in designing the capitalization of the new business. For example, shareholders may hold any of several classes or series of preferred stock or common stock, and there is no limitation on the number of shareholders. Start-up companies intending to engage in offering investment shares broadly to the public or obtain venture capital investments typically are structured as C corporations. In certain instances, however, an LLC or an S corporation may be a better choice so that early tax losses can flow through to the benefit of investors. Both LLCs and S corporations may be converted into C corporations, although there may be a tax cost related to doing so.

Shareholders of C corporations are not taxed on earnings of the corporation, but only on dividends and other distributions of cash or assets made by the corporation. Because the highest corporate tax rate is currently lower than the highest individual rate, and because most corporations are taxed at graduated rates, less total tax may be paid on earnings that are retained by a C corporation. This would be beneficial if the corporation will make few, if any, dividends or distributions during the growth stage of its business.

In contrast to LLCs, S corporations, and partnerships, C corporations are separate taxpayers. That is, the C corporations pay taxes on their own earnings, and shareholders pay a second time at ordinary rates on dividends that are usually at capital gains rates on the sale of C corporation stock. Unlike an S corporation shareholder, LLC member, or partner, a C corporation shareholder receives no direct tax benefit from tax losses incurred by the C corporation. When a C corporation distributes dividends to its shareholders assets that have appreciated in value, the shareholders would be taxed on the amount of appreciation.

Subchapter S Corporations

An S corporation is a corporation formed under state law just like a C corporation that has elected to be taxed under subchapter S of the Internal Revenue Code. The "S election" allows the corporation to avoid double taxation. Generally, an S corporation must satisfy each of the following: (1) it generally cannot be a foreign corporation; (2) it must have no more than 100 shareholders (although family members are counted as one owner); (3) each shareholder must be an individual, estate, or a specified type of trust; (4) no shareholder may be a nonresident alien (i.e., no corporations or partnerships may be owners); and (5) the corporation may have only one class of stock.

The main advantage of S corporation status is the avoidance of double taxation. Therefore, if it is structured properly, the S corporation is not taxed as a separate person. Federal Insurance Contribution Act (FICA) taxes may be minimized through payment of a reasonable salary to shareholder employees, with the remainder of the company's profits being distributed as dividends that are not subject to FICA or self-employment taxes.

FICA stipulates that there is a maximum that can be allocated to Social Security, while there is no maximum on what can go toward Medicare. Once the maximum to Social Security is achieved, the contributor's FICA payment will not increase the Social Security portion but will continue to increase the contribution to Medicare. The amount of the FICA payment depends on the income of the contributor: the higher the income, the higher the FICA payment. This point may be of significance if one decides to structure the ACO with shared employees between various physician practices.

S corporation owners who work for their business are employees. FICA is imposed only on wages paid to these owners. Although there may be a temptation to pay no wages since the owners must report all of their share of net income from the business for income tax purposes, the IRS does not espouse this practice. In fact, owners must receive (and pay FICA on) reasonable compensation for work performed. Making sure that S corporation owners do not skirt this rule has become a key audit target of the IRS.

The primary disadvantage of an S corporation is the lack of flexibility in structuring the company's capitalization. For example, many venture capital or private equity investors would not qualify as S corporation shareholders. Generally, S corporation capital structures are not as flexible as those of C corporations. S corporations may have only one class of stock. Venture capital funds and other institutional investors may not hold stock in an S corporation because only individuals, estates, and certain trusts may be shareholders in such entities.

A dividend or distribution by an S corporation of assets that have appreciated in value is a taxable event for the corporation's shareholders; a similar distribution by an LLC or partnership is generally not taxable. There is no step up in the tax basis of an S corporation's assets upon a sale of stock or the death of a shareholder, but such a step up can be achieved by an LLC that makes the appropriate election under the Internal Revenue Code.

S corporation shareholders do not include third-party debt in the tax basis of their shares, which limits the shareholder's tax benefit from such losses. Furthermore, an employee who receives S corporation stock is taxed immediately upon the receipt or the vesting of the shares. Be acutely aware that if an ACO starts out as an S corporation, and then one of the participant owners that joins happens to be a physician group practicing under one TIN, the ACO entity will lose its ability to be classified by the IRS as an S corporation.

Limited Liability Companies

Limited liability companies, or LLCs, are probably the most prevalent form of legal entity for new businesses as well as startup ACOs. An LLC has characteristics of both a corporation and a partnership. Like a corporation, an LLC affords its owners (also called members) solid limited-liability protection but allows them to design a flexible financial and management structure. Unlike a C corporation, an LLC is not taxed as a separate person and thus avoids double taxation. Moreover, like partners of a partnership, LLC members are able to claim the benefits of tax losses incurred by the company.

LLCs are very flexible by nature, allowing customized management and economic arrangements. Unlike an S corporation, there is no limitation on the type of entity that can be an owner or investor in an LLC. Because the LLC is a "pass-through entity" for tax purposes, LLC owners have only one level of taxation on profits and generally may claim LLC losses immediately on their individual tax returns. In contrast to limited partners of a partnership, LLC members enjoy the protection of limited liability even if they participate directly in management of the business. When structuring an ACO, it is always a good idea to have the corporate "flexibility" necessary to facilitate the multiple possible permutations needed to accommodate the needs of the physician provider group. The need to change corporate structure may be impacted by factors such as changes in regulation, changes in reimbursement, or even changes in the political or personal interactions/relationships between health care providers within the ACO.

An LLC may merge or consolidate with a corporation, a limited partnership or another LLC without any difficulty. Furthermore, contribution of equity or assets to an LLC can be accomplished more easily for tax purposes than with a corporation. Upon a sale of assets by an LLC, the purchaser may receive a "stepped-up basis" in the assets purchased, allowing the purchaser to enjoy greater depreciation deductions, while there is no tax at the LLC level on such gain. Unlike a C corporation (and sometimes an S corporation, where taxation of appreciated assets can be complicated), LLC owners are not subject to double taxation upon an LLC's dissolution and liquidation.

LLC owners who are also employees generally must pay self-employment taxes and make estimated tax payments. When structuring the physician-owned ACO, one can anticipate multiple health care provider participants with multiple TINs that come together as partial owners of the ACO. The physicians may choose to be equity investors, or the ACO may find a capital partner that is a nonphysician nonparticipant that may own as much as 25 percent of the ACO. One is likely to find that venture capital funds and institutional investors prefer to invest in corporations, but if the LLC is structured equitably and reasonably so as to satisfy both physician participant and nonparticipant equity partner, there is no reason not to achieve a mutually beneficial symbiosis. There are no limits on the type or number of owners in an LLC. For example, corporations can be LLC owners. In addition, an LLC may elect with the IRS to be treated as a C corporation, an S corporation, a partnership, or even a disregarded entity. LLC owners are self-employed individuals subject to self-employment tax (which covers both the employer and employee share of FICA for Social Security and Medicare taxes). Generally, owners must pay self-employment tax on their share of net earnings from the business.

Partnerships

Partnerships have been used for many years in all types of business relationships. A partnership can take the form of either a general partnership, which has only "general partners," or a limited partnership, which has both general partners and "limited partners." Limited partnerships provide limited liability protection to limited partners, subject to certain rules and restrictions, but every partnership must have at least one general partner who would be liable for all debts and liabilities of the partnership. Partnerships offer great flexibility in the design of a business's capital structure and also afford significant tax advantages to the partners. Because LLCs are able to offer similar flexibility and tax benefits without the necessity of one or more general partners, LLCs have largely superseded partnerships as a legal entity for many startup ventures—including ACOs.

Can the leaders readily list the ACO stakeholders and explain how each will contribute to patient care, quality improvement, and cost reduction? If not, the ACO is probably still too nascent to function well. Is the governing body representative of the organization? ACOs participating in the SSP are required to have beneficiary representation and at least 75 percent provider representation on the governing board. If the ACO includes employed and independent physicians or members of a participating independent practice association (IPA), both groups should be represented. If one is a family physician, his or her perspective would be useful to any ACO board. If one does not want that level of involvement, it is still valuable to know that the board of the ACO has strong family-medicine and other primary care representation.

Especially in ACOs that take commercial contracts, leaders should thoroughly comprehend where the ACO stands with respect to antitrust laws, Stark laws, anti-kickback laws, etc. The ACA does enable ACOs operating within the SSP to avoid such legal issues, but outside the SSP, things are different. As an organization of potentially independent providers contracting with payers, ACOs established without expert legal advice can run aground on any of them.

Do the leaders of the entity appreciate the potential for improved quality and reduced cost that primary care offers? If not, the ACO may be too stuck in outmoded styles of practice to succeed.

Historically, there was a time when IPAs were a popular form of physician structure for physician groups in the United States. An IPA is a group of physician practices that have a contractual agreement to work together to provide health care for patients in a health plan network or integrated system. The existing infrastructure, management, information technology and organizational expertise/elements are important building blocks to a

POACO. Unfortunately, when IPA entities began running afoul of certain antitrust laws, the IPA structure began losing favor with physicians.

An ACO developed by an IPA may be smaller and not as well capitalized than one based on an integrated delivery system; more challenged to develop a strong, centralized leadership and the kind of process standardization needed to maximize efficiency and quality; and more likely to appreciate the opportunities for quality improvement and cost reduction offered by primary care. In contrast, a hospital-led ACO or one developed by an integrated delivery system may be better capitalized, better managed, larger, and able to realize savings across a wider range of settings. On the other hand, the hospital-led ACO may also be too hospital-oriented; that is, it may spend more time and effort improving the quality and efficiency of hospital care than working to keep patients out of the hospital. Moreover, it may by stuck in the "traditional view" of primary care networks as referral channels funneling patients into the hospital.

An ACO that includes employed and aligned physicians may have different expectations of and for the two groups. If one is contemplating such an ACO, it is important to understand how the groups differ for primary care physicians and for referral specialists. The ACO may hire or include a management services organization to help with administrative functions. That is not a good or bad sign in itself, and it may indicate that the ACO recognizes the value of professional management.

One should be confident that the policies and procedures that will govern the ACO and influence the participating medical practices are ones that the participants can be comfortable with. Given that processes and workflows are likely to be standardized in an ACO, family physicians and other primary care physicians should be involved in the development of workflows, clinical policies, and policies in general—anything that affects primary care practice.

Even if one knows from the outset that patients are attributed to the ACO by virtue of where they get the largest proportion of their primary care, one will want to ask whether attribution is carried out prospectively or retrospectively. Prospective attribution uses claims data from previous years to determine patient attribution. This methodology allows the ACO to know up front which patients they will be held accountable for during a given year. On the other hand, it may count patients who do not meet inclusion criteria during the current year, who choose to receive the bulk of their care outside the ACO. This "leakage" can be a source of significant cost for the ACO and is a condition over which it has relatively little control.

In contrast, retrospective attribution assigns beneficiaries to an ACO at the end of a given year of ACO operation (a "performance year") by looking back over that year's data to see which patients qualified for attribution to the ACO during the year. This ensures that only patients who met the program criteria in the performance year are counted toward the ACO's attributed lives for that year. This methodology, however, means that the participant will not know whether any patient that participant sees will count until the end of the year. The SSP tries to balance the strengths of these respective methodologies by using a hybrid approach comprising a preliminary prospective attribution with updates during the year and a year-end retrospective reconciliation to count only those beneficiaries who met the attribution requirements for the whole year.

Patient attribution can be further complicated if the primary care physicians or other providers on whom attribution is based have some patients inside the ACO and some outside, or some in one ACO and some in another that contracts with the same payer. To avoid this problem, the SSP requires providers on whom attribution is based to be exclusive to one participating ACO, except under special circumstances.

Below is a list of critical questions that should be answered when structuring the ACO:

1. Which payers are represented in the ACO?
2. What quality and efficiency criteria must be met for the ACO to share in savings?
3. Does the ACO have an estimate of the shared savings it expects to earn? If so, on what assumptions is the estimate based?
4. Does the ACO have any contracts with downside risk?
5. How great a loss might it sustain?

The successful ACO is likely to distribute at least some of the savings in proportion to providers' contributions to value: care improvement and cost reduction. Shared savings can also be distributed based on percentage of attributed patients. That is, the physician who manages 5 percent of the patients in an ACO might be entitled to 5 percent of the savings. An ACO that has a hospital partner faces the question of how to divide savings fairly among the hospital and individual physicians; make sure to consider the division fair.

Whatever the ACO's distribution rationale, it is important to make sure that the compensation/distribution algorithm is written down and understood by each participant. When working with physicians, it is helpful to provide a conservative estimate of what the ACO expects that physicians' portion of the shared savings will be, if any. If the ACO accepts downside risk, it is important to relay how much risk each participant will be taking on. Having a clear articulation of this aspect will prevent much heartache of potential litigation from a physician participant—for many litigators will say that a physician plaintiff is a tenacious adversary.

Another crucial issue that must be addressed in the structure of the ACO is whether or not physicians will be required to buy into the entity. Depending on the share price, the buy-in cost may be a significant barrier to participation. However, it may also demonstrate the ACO's healthy awareness that startup requires significant capital. Whether or not there is a buy-in fee, it is important to understand how the ACO plans to fund all the infrastructure development it will need to succeed. Although CMS estimates startup costs to begin at as much as $1 million, this author's experience suggests that $1.5 to $2 million is a more realistic number.

Insurance companies or health plans may be important partners in any ACO structuring effort because the IT infrastructure available to these partners would be extremely valuable in facilitating data analysis and actuarial expertise that is necessary for ACO function. In the final analysis, the corporate structure of the ACO should be geared toward optimizing the governance, operations, and financial cash flow of the entity. Although this author favors the LLC as an ideal entity structure for an ACO, the critical point is that a truly patient-centered ACO should be physician-led in order to maximize the benefit to the patient.

Notes

1. 72 Fed. Reg 67801, 67815–16 (Nov. 2, 2011).
2. *Id.*
3. 76 Fed. Reg. at 67,815.
4. *Id.*
5. *Id.*
6. *Id.* at 67,816.
7. 42 C.F.R. § 425.204(d); 76 Fed. Reg. at 67,816.
8. 42 C.F.R. § 425.106(b)(4).
9. *Id.* § 425.106(b)(5).
10. 76 Fed. Reg. at 67,818.
11. 42 C.F.R. § 425.106(c)(1); 76 Fed. Reg. at 67,819.
12. 76 Fed. Reg. at 67,819.
13. *Id.*
14. *Id.* at 67,820.
15. *Id.*
16. 42 C.F.R. § 425.106(c)(2).
17. 76 Fed. Reg. at 67,820.
18. 42 C.F.R. § 425.106(c)(4).
19. *Id.* § 425.106(c)(5).
20. *Id.* § 425.106(d).
21. *Id.* § 425.108(a).
22. *Id.* § 425.108(b).
23. *Id.* § 425.108(c).
24. 76 Fed. Reg. at 67,823.
25. *Id.* at 67,823.
26. 42 C.F.R. § 425.108(d).
27. 76 Fed. Reg. at 67,824–25.
28. 42 C.F.R. § 425.108(e).
29. 76 Fed. Reg. at 67,823.
30. *Id.* at 67,823–24.
31. 42 C.F.R. § 425.204(c)(1)(iii).
32. *Id.* § 425.10; 76 Fed. Reg. at 67,806.
33. 42 C.F.R. § 425.20; 76 Fed. Reg. at 67,907.

34. 76 Fed. Reg. at 67,936.

35. G-code—"G-codes are HCPCS (Healthcare Common Procedural Coding System) codes that were developed to enable reporting of data for the calculation of quality measures. These codes supplement the usual claims data with clinical data that can be used to measure quality of services provided to beneficiaries. Each of the quality measures is assigned a G-code." William D. Rogers, MD, FACEP, *CMS' Medical Officer Explains PQRI,* p. 22, available at http://www.medicarepatientmanagement.com/issues/02-02/mpmMJ07-PQRI_Rogers.pdf.

36. 42 C.F.R. § 425.110(a)(1).

37. *Id.* § 425.110(2)(b).

38. *Id.* § 425.110(2)(b)(1).

39. *Id.* § 425.110(2)(b)(2).

40. *Id.* § 425.402; 76 Fed. Reg. at 67,857.

41. 42 C.F.R. § 425.400; 76 Fed. Reg. at 67,839, 67,836.

42. 76 Fed. Reg. at 67,806.

43. *Id.* at 67,806.

44. 42 C.F.R. § 425.316(b); 76 Fed. Reg. at 67,951.

45. 76 Fed. Reg. at 67,806.

46. *See* 42 C.F.R. § 425.102(a).

47. *Id.* § 425.20.

48. *Id.* § 425.102(b); 76 Fed. Reg. at 67,814.

49. 42 C.F.R. § 425.104(a).

9 The Accountable Care Organization Participant Agreement

Accountable Care Organizations (ACOs) that participate in the SSP must agree to a minimum three-year commitment to participate, memorialized in an ACO participant agreement. Because some providers may need to discontinue participation before three years, the Centers for Medicare and Medicaid Services (CMS) requires 60 days' notice of such intentions to discontinue the agreement or dissolve the ACO. CMS will retain any portion of a 25 percent withholding of the shared savings for ACOs in the event the ACOs' three-year agreement is terminated prematurely.

CMS finalized its proposal that the ACO participants must agree to the requirements set forth in the agreement between the ACO and CMS, sign a participation agreement, and submit the signed agreement to CMS.[1] However, CMS modified a number of the agreement requirements from the proposed rule, recognizing that a January 1, 2012, start date may not be feasible.[2] Specifically, CMS provides two options for start dates of the participation agreement in 2012: an April 1 start date or a July 1 start date.[3] The earlier start date has a longer performance period of 21 months; the latter has an 18-month performance period. Both performance periods ended on December 31, 2013. In both cases, the agreement term will be three performance periods, ending December 31, 2015.[4]

CMS reserves the right to modify agreement provisions and requirements during the term of the agreement.[5] ACOs will be responsible for all policy and SSP changes during the agreement, except for eligibility requirements regarding organization and governance of ACOs, determination of the sharing rate, and assignment of beneficiaries.[6] An ACO has the right to terminate its agreement if regulatory requirements are changed, if it feels those modifications will alter its ability to maintain participation in the SSP.[7] An ACO must include an adequate number of primary care providers for the number of assigned Medicare beneficiaries.[8] However, in its comments, CMS notes there were significant objections to its proposal that primary care physicians be exclusive to one ACO, on the grounds that "such exclusivity could be disruptive of their current practice patterns, which may involve the assignment of patients to a number of ACOs."[9]

CMS clarifies in the final rule that the primary care physician exclusivity requirement—that a primary care physician be exclusively affiliated with one ACO—only applies in situations where the provider is using its own tax identification number (TIN) to bill and forms the basis for beneficiary assignment.[10] Providers billing through different TINs of one or multiple group practices could participate in multiple ACOs. However, solo practitioners, both primary care and specialists, who provide primary care services upon which beneficiary assignment is based and who bill under their own personal TIN would need to be exclusive to a single ACO.[11]

The comments clarify that each ACO participant TIN upon which beneficiary assignment is dependent must be exclusive to one ACO.[12] CMS aims to "define the ACO operationally by its Medicare enrolled ACO participants' TINs."[13] CMS states that a large health system with one TIN cannot include only parts of the system in an ACO.[14] CMS also notes that this level of exclusivity of providers to an ACO is "necessary in order for the assignment process to function correctly, and especially to ensure the accurate assignment of beneficiaries to one and only one ACO."[15]

The final rule requires ACOs to submit both the TINs of all ACO participants and the national provider identification (NPI) numbers associated with ACO providers and suppliers.[16] Each ACO must maintain, update, and annually report to CMS those TINs and NPIs that are participants and providers/suppliers of the respective ACO.[17] CMS clarifies that this information is needed "in order to assign beneficiaries to ACOs appropriately and accurately."[18] CMS reserves the right to request additional information as part of the application process.[19]

In this author's experience, the most common reason that an ACO participant that is a medical practice group withdraws or is unable to participate for the duration of the ACO participant agreement term is medical-group practice instability due to operational or financial deficiencies. For example, a group may have taken out a large loan to start up its medical practice, and suddenly the reimbursement for a particular patient or procedure is unexpectedly decreased significantly—leaving the practice unable to manage cash flow sufficiently to meet their overhead expenses. Another reason may be that the group practice has experienced sudden growth and is operationally unable to manage its ancillary staff effectively in order to maximize the care delivered to an increased patient population.

With the widespread uncertainty being experienced by many in the medical profession, it is quite likely that CMS will make changes to the ACO regulations in future rule promulgations. During the three-year contract, ACOs will be subject to all regulation changes, with the exception of eligibility requirements concerning the governance of ACOs, the calculation of the sharing rate, and assignment of beneficiaries. Therefore, ACOs would have to comply with any changes related to quality performance standards. For these and other required changes, ACOs would have to submit a supplement to their original application explaining how they propose to address them, or face a corrective action plan and potential termination.

An ACO may also initiate changes during the three-year contract period. Changes to ACO provider composition are of particular concern. To avoid antitrust violations that could result in ACO termination, CMS proposes that an ACO may not add providers during the three-year agreement. However, ACOs would be allowed to remove providers. An ACO must give CMS 30 days' notice of such action, and CMS will determine whether the ACO will have to terminate, start over, continue as is, or be subject to a new antitrust review.

Each ACO will be required to submit a tax identification number (TIN) and a national provider identification (NPI) number for each participating provider and to update these numbers annually. This information will support beneficiary assignment and allow CMS to create data reports tailored to ACO-specific populations. There should be no confusion as to the definition of who an ACO participant is.[20] CMS will make available aggregated data reports on the ACO populations at the beginning of the first performance period and then on a quarterly basis. This includes doing so in conjunction with yearly financial and quality performance reports used to assess performance.

When an ACO completes an SSP application, the applicant is required to submit samples of the agreements that are in force between the ACO and the ACO participants (including their TINs), the ACO provider/suppliers, and other entities furnishing services or performing functions related to ACO activities. In addition, the applicant will also be required to submit the first and last pages of the agreements that each of the ACO participants that have joined to form the ACO have executed.

The regulations require certain elements to be included in the ACO participant agreement. If those elements are not present, the agreement must be rejected for not meeting program requirements. It is critically important for the parties to the agreement to be clearly identified as the ACO legal entity and the ACO participant legal entity. Any lack of clarity or a mismatch between the ACO participant agreement and the submitted ACO participant list can result in rejection of the ACO's application.

All ACO participants and ACO providers/suppliers must agree to comply with the requirements and conditions of the program as well as all laws regulations set forth in 42 C.F.R. Part 425.[21] The ACO participant agreement should clearly identify the parties entering into the agreement, the agreement date, and the length of agreement. Other crucial items to include in the agreement are the following:

- The agreement is directly between the ACO legal entity and the ACO participant (TIN). (Please review the Shared Savings Program definition of an ACO participant at § 425.20.)
- The correct legal entity name of both the ACO and ACO participant and that these legal entity names are used consistently throughout the document. The applicant will be asked to re-execute the agreement if the legal entity names do not match the legal entity names on record for

the TINs of both organizations. For example, the introduction should appear as something like the following:

> This ACO Participant Agreement ("Agreement") is by and between Startup ACO of America, L.L.C. dba Startup ACO ("ACO"), and ABC Group Practice P.C. ("ACO Participant") and is effective [Month, Day, Year] ("Effective Date").

The ACO participant agreement must include a requirement to comply with the Medicare SSP requirements and all applicable laws and regulations, including HIPAA. In addition, the agreement should identify the rights and obligations of the parties, including whether, how, and under what circumstances shared savings will be distributed. The agreement should include standard provisions governing issues including, but not limited to, defined terms, ACO obligations, ACO participant obligations, and termination.

The ACO is responsible for ensuring that all ACO providers/suppliers (NPIs) that bill through the TIN of the ACO participant have also agreed to participate in the SSP and follow program regulations. The ACO may ensure this by having direct agreements with each ACO provider/supplier (NPI) or indirectly through its agreement with the ACO participant TIN. If the ACO chooses to require the ACO participant to ensure that each ACO provider/supplier has agreed to participate, consider including language in the ACO Participant agreement that clearly requires the ACO participant to do so.

Each agreement must include a signature page that is signed by individuals who have the legal authority to bind the party on whose behalf they are signing the agreement. The signature page must reflect information for both the ACO and the ACO participant and should be consistent with the legal entity names listed on the first page of the agreement. Information other than the signature should be typed for easy reference and readability. It is strongly encouraged to include the following information in the recommended format on the next page.

Sample Signature Page (Recommended Format)

IN WITNESS WHEREOF, the parties have caused this Agreement to be executed by the duly authorized representatives as of the dates below

For the ACO:

____

Legal Entity Name

____

d/b/a Name

____

Signature (on behalf of the ACO)

____

Name

____

Title

____

Date

____

Address

____

City, State Zip Code

____

Business Phone

____

Business Fax

According to the regulations and resources/guidelines available through www.cms.gov, the four main elements required in the ACO Participant Agreement are

1. "An explicit requirement that the ACO participant or the ACO provider/supplier will comply with the requirements and conditions of the Medicare Shared Savings Program (42 C.F.R. Part 425), including, but not limited to, those specified in the participation agreement with CMS."

2. The ACO participants and ACO providers/suppliers rights and obligations in and representation by the ACO.
3. How the opportunity to get shared savings or other financial arrangements will encourage ACO participants and ACO providers/suppliers to adhere to the quality assurance and improvement program and evidence-based clinical guidelines.
4. Remedial measures that will apply to ACO participants and ACO providers/suppliers in the event of noncompliance with the requirements of their agreements with the ACO.

Examples

Correct: A large group practice decides to participate in an ACO. Its owner signs an agreement on behalf of the practice to participate in the program and follow program regulations. Also, all practitioners that have reassigned their billings to the TIN of the large group practice have also agreed to participate and follow program regulations. The ACO may include this group practice TIN on its list of ACO participants.

Incorrect: A large group practice decides to participate in an ACO. Its owner signs an agreement to participate in the program and follow program regulations. However, not all practitioners that have reassigned their billings to the TIN of the large group practice have agreed to participate and follow program regulations. The ACO may not include this group practice TIN on its list of ACO participants.

Incorrect: Several practitioners in a large group practice decide to participate in an ACO. However, the group practice as a whole has not agreed to participate in the program. The ACO may not include this group practice TIN on its list of ACO participants.

Exhibit 1 is included at the end of this chapter and was developed by the author to comply with the regulations. Please note that—depending upon the type of corporate structure of the ACO as well as compensation/distribution scheme outlined in its operating agreement/partnership as a general guideline representative of an agreement that has passed CMS scrutiny.

Notes

1. 42 C.F.R. § 425.200(b)–(c); 76 Fed. Reg. 67,801, 67,811.
2. 76 Fed. Reg. at 67,836.
3. *Id.*
4. *Id.*
5. 42 C.F.R. § 425.212.
6. *Id.* § 425.212(2).
7. *Id.* § 425.212(2)(d).
8. *Id.* § 425.110(a)(1).
9. 76 Fed. Reg. at 67,810.
10. *Id.* at 67,810.
11. 42 C.F.R. § 425.204(c)(5)(i).
12. 76 Fed. Reg. at 67,810–11.
13. 42 C.F.R. § 425.20; 76 Fed. Reg. at 67,809.
14. 76 Fed. Reg. at 67,816.
15. *Id.*
16. 42 C.F.R. § 425.204(c)(5)(i).
17. 76 Fed. Reg. at 67,809.
18. *Id.*
19. 42 C.F.R. § 455.205(c)(5)(i)(B)(ii).
20. *See* 42 C.F.R. § 425.20.
21. *See id.* §§ 425.204(c)(1)(i), 425.210.

Exhibit 1: Sample ACO Participation Agreement

STARTUP ACO OF AMERICA, LLC

PROVIDER PARTICIPATION AGREEMENT

This Agreement is effective on this ______ day of ____________, 20____ and is made by and between Startup ACO of America, L.L.C., a ___(State)________ limited liability company ("Startup ACO") and the undersigned Physician ("Provider").

1. Startup ACO is an accountable care organization ("ACO") formed by a partnership of the Primary Care and Specialist Provider community and Startup ACO. Providers are eligible to participate in the Startup ACO if they are members of the Startup ACO of America, LLC.
2. Startup ACO contracts with health benefit plans, employers and third party administrators ("Plans") to arrange for the provision of health care services to enrollees of those Plans in a manner that fosters the high quality and cost-effective delivery of health care services.
3. Startup ACO contracts with health care providers, including Provider, to provide primary care and specialty Provider services and other health care services to Plan enrollees.
4. Provider is a duly licensed physician in the State of __________ with board eligibility or board certification appropriate for Provider's specialty of practice, and Provider wishes to contract with Startup ACO to provide Provider services to Plan enrollees.
5. Provider understands that an "ACO participant" means an individual or a group of ACO providers/suppliers that are identified by a Medicare-enrolled Tax Identification Number ("TIN") that alone or together with one or more other ACO participants comprises the ACO. An ACO participant is identified at the billing TIN level, and

an ACO provider/supplier is a practitioner billing through the ACO participant's TIN.

6. Provider understands that all ACO providers/suppliers billing through an ACO participant TIN are included in the ACO by virtue of their relationship to the ACO participant and the ACO participant's relationship with the ACO.
7. The parties understand that all ACO providers/suppliers associated with each ACO participant TIN have agreed and will comply with the program regulations, and that an ACO may not include an entity as an ACO participant unless all providers and suppliers billing under that entity's billing TIN have agreed to participate.

In consideration of the mutual promises set forth below, Startup ACO and Provider agree as follows:

1. Medicare Shared Savings Program. Provider agrees to participate in and comply with all the requirements and conditions of 42 C.F.R. Part 425 of the Medicare Shared Savings Program, including but not limited to, those provisions specified in the participation agreement with CMS.

2. Rights and Obligations. Each ACO participant Provider shall become familiarized with all participants' and ACO providers'/suppliers' rights and obligations in and representation by the ACO, which are outlined in this Agreement and in the Startup ACO Policies and Procedures.

3. Incentives to Adhere to ACO Policies and Procedures. The opportunity for each provider to earn shared savings or other financial arrangements shall incentivize ACO participants and ACO providers/suppliers to adhere to the quality assurance and improvement program and evidence-based clinical guidelines described in the ACO Policies and Procedures. In addition, the ACO shall have the authority to terminate an ACO participant for non-compliance with this Agreement or any of the requirements of 42 C.F.R. part 425.

4. Participation with Startup ACO. Startup does not require that beneficiaries be referred to ACO participants or ACO providers/suppliers or to any other provider or supplier (pursuant to 42 C.F.R. 425.304(c)(2)), except under the specific and limited circumstances expressly permitted by the regulations. Subject to the terms and conditions of this

Agreement, Provider agrees to participate as a participating Provider of Startup ACO and to abide by the terms and conditions of this Agreement, its attached Exhibits, and the Operating Agreement of Startup ACO of America, LLC.

5. Remedial Measures. Remedial measures described in this Agreement and the Startup ACO Policies and Procedures shall apply to ACO participants and ACO providers/suppliers who do not adhere to the requirements of this Agreement.

6. ACO Governing Body. In compliance with 42 C.F.R. 425.106, the managing members of Startup shall have the authority to execute the functions of the CO. The managers shall have responsibility for oversight and strategic direction, holding the ACO management accountable for the ACO's activities. The managing members shall have a fiduciary duty to the ACO and must act consistent with that fiduciary duty.

7. Startup ACO Programs. Provider agrees to participate fully in all programs of Startup ACO relating to care protocols, quality assurance, utilization management, shared savings programs, peer review, credentialing, member grievance programs, or other professional programs established by Startup ACO. Provider may also exercise the option for Startup ACO to handle all revenue cycle management ("RCM") functions, but exercise of this option is not a requirement for membership. In addition, Provider agrees to accept any decisions relating to Provider and Provider's participation with Startup ACO, including corrective action, subject to all appeal rights as may be provided by each Plan or Startup ACO.

8. Eligibility for Ownership in Startup ACO. Provider shall be entitled to receive one hundred (100) Units of Membership Interest in Startup ACO upon execution of this agreement and submission of one dollar ($1.00) made payable to Startup ACO of America, LLC. Provider must agree to the terms and conditions of the Startup ACO Operating Agreement, attached as Exhibit "A."

However, if Provider Group becomes a member of Startup ACO, Group shall be eligible to receive one hundred (100) Units of Membership Interest per Provider partner or member of the Group. EXAMPLE: __________ Medical Group, P.A. has five (5) Provider shareholders, and wants to become a member of Startup ACO. Each Provider in the group pays

Startup ACO $1.00 apiece, and the Group is issued five hundred (500) Units of Membership Interest.

9. Plan Participation. At Provider's discretion, Provider may participate in any Plan(s) with which Startup ACO has a contract, subject to plan participation requirements. Provider understands and agrees that Startup ACO does not guarantee that Provider will be offered the opportunity to participate in each Plan under contract with Startup ACO. Provider agrees to comply with the terms and conditions of any agreements made by Startup ACO with such Plans and with Plan's applicable terms of participation, policies and procedures. Provider understands that Startup ACO shall make available a list of available plans once ACO certification is verified. The addition of such plans will not be considered an amendment of this agreement.

Provider understands and acknowledges that, by entering into this Agreement, Startup ACO members may be included as a Participating Provider in any or all of the Plans negotiated by Startup ACO. Provider understands and acknowledges that 1) such Plans may include both Plans where Eligible Person are offered a network of Participating Providers and Plans where Eligible Persons are not offered a network of Participating Providers; and 2) depending on the applicable Plan, Covered Services may be covered under the Eligible Person's in-network or out-of-network benefit. Notwithstanding anything to the contrary set forth in this Agreement, any professional liability exposure to a Provider is limited only to the Provider that provided or supervised the professional health care services rendered.

10. Agreement to Provide Services. Provider shall provide services that are within Provider's area of medical practice to Plan enrollees, subject to the terms and provisions of this Agreement and the coverage conditions of each Plan. Provider agrees not to discriminate against any enrollee on any basis prohibited by state or federal law or regulation.

11. Compensation. Payment for Covered Services under this Agreement is the sole responsibility of the third-party payer and shall be the lesser of Provider Members' usual billed charges or the reimbursement amount provided by the respective Payers, subject to applicable claim coding and bundling rules (if any) and minus applicable Copayments. Payments under this Agreement will be directed to the individual Member Provider and his/her associated tax identification number (TIN). The rates in this Agreement

will be payment in full for all services furnished to Eligible Persons under this Agreement. Except when coordination of benefits applies, undisputed amounts due and owing under this Agreement for a clean claim (as defined under applicable law) for Covered Services will be payable within thirty (30) days of receipt of such clean claim by the applicable Payer or Payer designee or within the timeframe required by the applicable state's prompt payment of claims law. Subject to the terms of the applicable Payer Agreement, if payment is not made within such timeframe, Provider member may elect not to extend the discount under this Agreement but only if Group or the Member Provider requests an adjustment to the claim with the applicable Payer within sixty (60) days of receipt of payment.

12. Notification of Changes to Members. Provider shall provide Startup ACO with at least thirty (30) days written notice of the addition of new Providers to his/her practice group, and sixty (60) days advance written notice if a Member Provider shall cease to provide Covered Services to Eligible Persons under this Agreement. Notwithstanding the foregoing, in the event the Member Provider's participation under this Agreement is terminated for cause and his/her group cannot provide such sixty (60) days advance notice, Provider shall notify Startup ACO in writing of such termination as soon as possible but no later than five (5) days after learning of such termination. Upon termination, Provider Member shall surrender their Unit(s) of Membership Interest pursuant to a Membership Interest Redemption Agreement back to Startup ACO.

13. Member Provider Agreements. Provider represents and warrants that it is authorized to act on behalf of his/her Group or individual practice, and Provider shall provide evidence of such authority upon request. To the extent that some Groups may have Providers that are not employed by Group, but are independently contracted with Group, Group shall maintain agreements with such Represented Providers requiring the Represented Providers to comply with the terms and conditions of this Agreement as well as the Startup ACO Operating Agreement to the extent applicable and to accept payment for Covered Services upon the terms and conditions set forth in this Agreement. The form of Group's standard agreement with such Member Providers shall contain all provisions required by applicable law and shall include a hold harmless provision

acceptable to Startup ACO and consistent with applicable law. Such form and any material amendments thereto must be approved in advance by Startup ACO, which approval shall not be unreasonably withheld. Upon request, Group or individual Provider shall make available to Startup ACO and to any applicable regulatory authority a copy of each such Member Provider agreement.

14. Policies and Procedures. Provider agrees to comply with (i) all policies and procedures of Startup ACO, (ii) all applicable government program requirements, and (iii) all Plan requirements.

15. Maintenance of License and Staff Privileges. Provider shall maintain in good standing all licenses, registrations, certifications, and/or privileges as required by Startup ACO and each Plan to render services to enrollees. Provider shall immediately notify Startup ACO of any change in Provider's license, certification or privileges on any medical staff.

16. Compliance with Laws. Provider shall comply will all applicable federal, state and local laws and regulations, including without limitation all Medicare and Medicaid statutes and regulations.

17. Claims. Provider shall submit claims to Plan(s) on designated claim forms within the time period required by the applicable Plan. Provider acknowledges that the failure to submit accurate, complete and clean claims as required by a Plan within the required time period may render such claims not payable.

18. Hold Harmless. Provider agrees that claims for services rendered to enrollees shall be paid to Provider directly by each Plan. Provider agrees to look solely to Plan for payment for services provided by Provider to Plan enrollees, which are covered by Plan. Provider agrees not to bill, charge, collect a deposit from, seek compensation from, or have any recourse against any enrollee, except to the extent that Plan permits Provider to collect copayments, deductibles, coinsurance or payment for non-covered services directly from enrollees. Provider acknowledges and agrees that Startup ACO shall have no financial liability to Provider for payments for services provided to enrollees.

19. Insurance. Provider shall maintain professional liability insurance with minimum limits of coverage as required by Startup ACO or any Plan with which Startup ACO contracts, shall provide evidence of such coverage to

Startup ACO when requested, and shall notify Startup ACO immediately of any material changes or termination of coverage. Provider agrees to indemnify, defend and hold harmless Startup ACO and its members, managers, officers, employees, agents and lawyers from all liability, damages, claims, amounts, costs and expenses (including reasonable lawyers' fees) arising from the furnishing of medical services by Provider.

20. Confidentiality. Provider agrees to comply with the Health Insurance Portability and Accountability Act of 1996 and to maintain the confidentiality of enrollees' health information, enrollment information and financial terms of this Agreement and shall not release any such information except in compliance with applicable legal requirements or the written consent of the enrollee and Startup ACO. Provider agrees to execute the Business Associate Agreement, attached as Exhibit "B."

21. Maintenance and Access to Records. Provider agrees to prepare, maintain and retain medical, fiscal and administrative medical records for all services provided to enrollees in accordance with generally accepted medical practice and Startup ACO policies. Provider further agrees that Startup ACO shall have the right to audit and have access to Provider's records on reasonable notice and during normal business hours, for purposes of determining Provider's compliance with this Agreement and with applicable law.

22. Term and Termination. This Agreement shall remain in effect unless and until terminated as follows:

(a) By Provider or Startup ACO at any time with or without cause upon sixty (60) days' prior written notice to the other party;
(b) By Provider or Startup ACO upon a material breach of any term or condition of this Agreement upon twenty (20) days' written notice, provided that the breaching party shall have such twenty (20) day notice period to cure or resolve the breach and provided further, that such termination shall be subject to applicable Startup ACO appeal procedures;
(c) Immediately upon termination of Provider's membership interest in Startup ACO; or
(d) Immediately, in the event of the dissolution of Startup ACO, pursuant to the terms of the Startup ACO Operating Agreement.

23. Effect of Termination. Termination of this Agreement shall not relieve Provider of any obligations to enrollees currently receiving treatment and of all obligations that have accrued as of termination or which survive termination. Provider shall cooperate with Startup ACO, Plan and enrollees to ensure that enrollees are transferred to another Provider for treatment.

24. Miscellaneous.

(a) This Agreement contains the full and complete agreement of the parties relative to its subject matter.

(b) This Agreement may be amended only by a written agreement signed by both parties, except that Startup ACO may unilaterally amend this Agreement to comply with any legal requirements.

(c) This Agreement may not be assigned by either party without the written consent of the other party.

(d) In the performance of their respective duties and obligations hereunder, the relationship of the parties is that of independent contractors. Nothing in this Agreement shall be construed or be deemed to create any other relationship, including one of employment, agency or joint venture.

(e) This Agreement shall be governed by the laws of the State of __________.

IN WITNESS WHEREOF, the parties have duly executed this Provider Participation Agreement as of the dates set forth below.

STARTUP ACO OF AMERICA, LLC:

By: By:	______
Printed Name:	Printed Name:
Title: Manager	Title: Manager
Date:	Date:

PROVIDER OR GROUP PARTICIPANT:

By:

Printed Name:

Title:

Date:

Individual NPI#:______________________

ACO Participant TIN:__________________

Exhibit A
Startup ACO of America, LLC
Operating Agreement
(Attached)
Exhibit B
Startup ACO of America, LLC
Business Associate Agreement

For the ACO PARTICIPANT:

____
Legal Entity Name

____
d/b/a Name

____
ACO Participant TIN

____
Signature (on behalf of the ACO Participant)

____
Name

____
Title

____
Date

____
Address

____
City, State Zip Code

____
Business Phone

____
Business Fax

Medical Ethics and Accountable Care Organizations

10

Introduction

The practice of medicine has always been considered a noble profession, due primarily to the principle stated in the American Medical Association (AMA) Code of Medical Ethics Opinion 8.03: "Under no circumstances may physicians place their own financial interests above the welfare of their patients. The primary objective of the medical profession is to render service to humanity; reward or financial gain is a subordinate consideration." This passage from Opinion 8.03 also delineates a particular problem for which there is no real solution. Concern for the patient is almost always in competition with financial considerations. It is one thing for the physician or hospital to place the patient's welfare above their own interest; but what about the interests of third-party payers—and now with ACO Shared Savings Programs, the interests of fellow members?

Health insurance, as an employee benefit, developed out of the World War II economy. It became an entitlement to the elderly and certain of the poor in 1965, with the passage of Medicare and Medicaid. Trouble arises when there is no limit on utilization, which has threatened the continued viability of the entire system. While the medical profession has never wavered from the principle that the welfare of the patient must come first, ethics becomes much more complicated when a secondary consideration is the survival of the public and private social safety net and, now, consideration for fellow members of an Accountable Care Organization (ACO).

For example, one attempt to limit utilization is the idea of "coinsurance." While a person may be covered by insurance, the patient is responsible for a copayment component and the deductible amount. This could lead to conflict between the duty to the patient and the duty to the system. There is an ethics rule for just such a situation. American Medical Association (AMA) Opinion 6.12, Forgiveness or Waiver of Insurance Copayments:

- "Physicians commonly forgive or waive copayments to facilitate patient access to needed medical care. When a copayment is a barrier to needed care because of financial hardship, physicians should forgive or waive the copayment."
- "Physicians should be aware that forgiveness or waiver of copayments may violate the policies of some insurers, both public and private. . . . Routine forgiveness or waiver of copayments may constitute fraud under state and federal law."[1]

In sum, physicians may forgive copayments, but they may violate duties to others if they do this too often. Exactly what kind of trouble practitioners may encounter from unmet expectations isn't entirely clear. What separates fraud, unethical behavior, and simple unmet expectations isn't easy to define. In contractual dealings with patients and third parties, physicians and hospitals are expected to not only respect the needs of the patient but also respect the policies of the third-party payer, as well as promises made in contracts. What we can take from this as a matter of ethics is that providers have at least two concerns: (1) an ethical duty to take care of patients on an individualized basis and (2) a contractual and social responsibility to other interested parties.

Ignoring promises made to third parties, even in the name of patient care, is more and more frequently landing physicians and hospitals in very deep trouble. Providers have been subjected to the U.S. Department of Health and Human Services, Office of the Inspector General fraud investigations, private insurance audits, state and federal lawsuits, and medical board ethics complaints over the failure to meet expectations of conflicting interest groups. All seem to be attacking providers over financial matters. Organizations normally do not bite the hand that feeds them, unless there is nothing else to eat. As money becomes scarce, they are learning to do just that. In the case of the example of forgiveness of copayments, after trying everything else, insurance companies finally began earnestly requesting proof that patient copayments are not being routinely forgiven. In the absence of the ability to prove copayments are being collected, a provider may be reported to an ethics panel, charged with fraud by the Office of Inspector General, or a provider may receive a recoupment letter demanding return of insurance benefits paid.

Unpleasant business decisions have hardened attitudes, which may very well carry over into ACO administration. Lack of funds also taught parties how to read a code of medical ethics with the intention of finding a way to avoid payment or obligations. It is therefore more important than ever to understand that every decision may have ethical consequences. ACOs will add a layer of complexity to this problem, simply because there will be more contracts concerning previously unknown combinations of entities. The Affordable Care Act contained section 3022, which directed the Secretary of the Department of Health and Human Services to create a shared savings program—that is, ACOs—for Medicare. This legal framework was subsequently detailed by the Center for Medicare and Medicaid Services (CMS) as a final rule in November 2011.[2] Although a number of privately organized and successful accountable organizations exist, describing ACOs under Medicare is a new creature involving many diverse interests. There will be more expectations to be met, very serious questions as to control and distribution of shared savings, and, finally, parties that are likely to be partners in ACO contracts that historically do not like each other.

The Medicare ACO Shared Savings Program in General

The Medicare Shared Savings Program (SSP) allows any physician, hospital, physician network, and other health care provider group that cares for more than 5,000 Medicare fee-for-service beneficiaries to form an ACO and apply to participate.[3] Agreements last at least three years. The incentive to participate is the "shared savings" that the organization can earn if Medicare expenditures for its beneficiaries are less than the CMS benchmark calculated for that ACO. This incentive should stimulate ACOs to provide better-coordinated, higher-quality care while reducing expenses.[4] Under a one-sided-risk model, the ACO shares savings but suffers no loss if its expenditures are higher than the benchmark; under a two-sided-risk model, the ACO can share a greater portion of the savings at the risk of having to pay back a portion of Medicare's losses if its expenditures are higher than the benchmark. Both models require an ACO to report and meet 33 national quality measures. ACOs have significant freedom to adopt and create their own quality, efficiency, and patient care coordination interventions.

Governance and Ethics

Of course, the question of governance of ACOs will generate conflicts. Participation is not limited to doctors and hospitals. In many states, corporate practice-of-medicine statutes are strong, and ACOs may in fact violate such statutes. The final rule does not address this conflict, other than to state that federal law does not supersede state law.[5] In fact, the federal government probably lacks the power to supersede state police powers. Adding to the problem, the idea of mixing non-medically-licensed entities with doctors and hospitals to form an entity that will make health care decisions is anathema to the AMA and other conservative physician groups. Not surprisingly, when the AMA House of Delegates met in 2010, members established a set of "Accountable Care Organization Principles" and the organization heavily favored physician autonomy and governance: "ACOs must be physician-led to ensure that a physician's medical decisions are not based on commercial interests, but rather on professional medical judgment that puts patients' interests first."[6]

Acceptance of ACOs by Beneficiaries and Acceptance of Beneficiaries by ACOs

The final rule[7] adopted November 11, 2011, section 1899(b)(2)(A) of the act, requires participating ACOs to "be willing to become accountable for the quality, cost, and overall care of the Medicare fee-for-service beneficiaries assigned to it." The Department of Health and Human Services stated in the proposed final rule, "to satisfy this requirement, we proposed that an ACO executive who has the authority to bind the ACO must certify to the best of his or her knowledge, information, and belief that the ACO participants are willing to become accountable for, and to report to us on, the quality, cost, and overall care of the Medicare [fee-for-service] beneficiaries assigned to the ACO." This led to objections during the comment period that certain patients may be unmanageable. Would the ACO members be forced to accept these patients?

The Secretary of Health and Human Services replied in the final rule, "In order to retain beneficiary freedom of choice under traditional [fee-for-service] Medicare, the basis for beneficiary assignment to ACOs is where, and from whom, they choose to receive a plurality of their primary care services during the performance year." In other words, yes, the patient gets to choose, even if they are unmanageable. Further, "ACOs must be willing to become accountable for total quality, cost, and overall care of these Medicare [fee-for-service] beneficiaries," apparently regardless of whether the ACO members wish to take on the patient. The final rule comments continue, "An ACO will not receive an assignment of those beneficiaries that choose not to receive care from ACO providers." However, "beneficiaries who choose to receive care from ACO providers, regardless of whether they are 'unmanageable' or noncompliant with treatment recommendations may become part of the ACO's assigned population." The Secretary continues with a condescending statement that physicians groups find infuriating: "Since patient-centeredness is an integral part of this program, we believe such beneficiaries represent an excellent opportunity for ACOs to create, implement, and improve upon patient-centered processes that improve patient engagement." The Secretary ended with a threat: "We note that avoidance of such beneficiaries, as described in more detail in section II.H.3. of this final rule, will result in termination of an ACO's participation agreement."[8]

Ethics in Referrals between Members of an ACO

The AMA takes the position that physician and patient participation in an ACO should be voluntary and that patient participation in an ACO should be voluntary, rather than a mandatory assignment to an ACO by Medicare. Unlike health maintenance organizations, ACOs claim to allow patient choice of doctors (especially under Medicare's rules), but evidence suggests that cost savings might depend on the ACO's control over referral patterns.[9] Paramount, however, is the idea that a physician referral is needed for most any service paid for by Medicare and Medicaid. Referrals may not be made simply because a specialist or hospital participates in the SSP. There is an additional ethical step:

AMA Opinion 3.04: Referral of Patients[10]

> A physician may refer a patient for diagnostic or therapeutic services to another physician, limited practitioner, or any other provider of health care services permitted by law to furnish such services, whenever he or she believes that this may benefit the patient. As in the case of referrals to physician-specialists, referrals to limited practitioners should be based on their individual competence and ability to perform the services needed by the patient. A physician should not so refer a patient unless the physician is confident that the services provided on referral will be performed competently and in accordance with accepted scientific standards and legal requirements.

Hospital-led ACOs are actually in a better position, however, to run an ACO, for any of a number of reasons. Primarily, hospitals are accustomed to managing complicated relationships. Hospital-led ACOs may in fact become the dominant model if current trends continue. This will probably lead to frustration and perhaps dysfunction, which could spill over into ethical allegations.

A number of existing ethics opinions are relevant to ACOs and SSP concepts. The two most directly analogous opinions deal with pay-for-performance programs and conflicts of interest under capitation.

AMA Ethics Opinion 8.056: Physician Pay-for-Performance Programs

Physician pay-for-performance (PFP) compensation arrangements should be designed to improve health care quality and patient safety by linking remuneration to measures of individual, group, or organizational performance. To uphold their ethical obligations, physicians who are involved with PFP programs must take appropriate measures to promote patients' well-being.

1. Physicians who are involved in the design or implementation of PFP programs should advocate for
   a. incentives that are intended to promote health care quality and patient safety, and are not primarily intended to contain costs;
   b. program flexibility that allows physicians to accommodate the varying needs of individual patients;
   c. adjustment of performance measures by risk and case-mix in order to avoid discouraging the treatment of high-risk individuals and populations; and
   d. processes to make practice guidelines and explanations of their intended purposes and the clinical findings upon which they are based available to participating physicians.
2. Practicing physicians who participate in PFP programs while providing medical services to patients should
   a. maintain primary responsibility to their patients and provide competent medical care, regardless of financial incentives;
   b. support access to care for all people and avoid selectively treating healthier patients for the purpose of bolstering their individual or group performance outcomes;
   c. be aware of evidence-based practice guidelines and the findings upon which they are based;

d. always provide care that considers patients' individual needs and preferences, even if that care conflicts with applicable practice guidelines; and

e. not participate in PFP programs that incorporate incentives that conflict with physicians' professional values or otherwise compromise physicians' abilities to advocate for the interests of individual patients.

Opinion 8.051: Conflicts of Interest under Capitation

The application of capitation to physicians' practices can result in the provision of cost-effective, quality medical care. It is important to note, however, that the potential for conflict exists under such systems. Physicians who contract with health care plans should attempt to minimize these conflicts and to ensure that capitation is applied in a manner consistent with patients' interests.

1. Physicians have an obligation to evaluate a health plan's capitation payments prior to contracting with that plan to ensure that the quality of patient care is not threatened by inadequate rates of capitation. Physicians should advocate that capitation payments be calculated primarily on the basis of relevant medical factors, available outcomes data, the costs associated with involved providers, and consensus-oriented standards of necessary care. Furthermore, the predictable costs resulting from existing conditions of enrolled patients should be considered when determining the rate of capitation. Different populations of patients have different medical needs, and the costs associated with those needs should be reflected in the per-member, per-month payment. Physicians should seek agreements with plans that provide sufficient financial resources for all care that is the physician's obligations to deliver and should refuse to sign agreements that fail in this regard.
2. Physicians must not assume inordinate levels of financial risk and should therefore consider a number of factors when deciding whether or not to sign a provider agreement. The size of the plan and the time period over which the rate is figured should be considered by physicians evaluating a plan as well as in determinations of the per-member, per-month payment. The capitation rate for large plans

can be calculated more accurately than for smaller plans because of the mitigating influence of probability and the behavior of large systems. Similarly, length of time will influence the predictability of the cost of care. Therefore, physicians should advocate for capitation rates calculated for large plans over an extended period of time.

3. Stop-loss plans can prevent the potential of catastrophic expenses from influencing physician behavior. Physicians should ensure that such arrangements are finalized prior to signing an agreement to provide services in a health plan.
4. Physicians must be prepared to discuss with patients any financial arrangements that could impact patient care. Physicians should avoid reimbursement systems that, if disclosed to patients, could negatively affect the patient-physician relationship.

Relation to State Laws

It is important to understand that even though the fact that ACO SSPs are authorized by law, such authorization does not supersede rules relating to medical ethics. Section 1.02 of the AMA Code of Medical Ethics makes clear:

> Ethical values and legal principles are usually closely related, but ethical obligations typically exceed legal duties. In some cases, the law mandates unethical conduct. In general, when physicians believe a law is unjust, they should work to change the law. In exceptional circumstances of unjust laws, ethical responsibilities should supersede legal obligations.

Thus, under existing ethics opinions, to uphold their ethical obligations, physicians who are involved with ACO Shared Savings Programs must take appropriate measures to promote patients' well-being. This may include the following:

- The ACO must be operated in a manner in which incentives intended to promote health care quality and patient safety and are not primarily intended to contain costs.

- The ACO must support access to care for all people and avoid selectively treating healthier patients for the purpose of bolstering their individual or group performance outcomes.
- The ACO program should maintain flexibility that allows physicians to accommodate the varying needs of individual patients.
- Physicians should not participate in programs that incorporate incentives that conflict with physicians' professional values or otherwise compromise physicians' abilities to advocate for the interests of individual patients.
- Physicians have an obligation to evaluate an ACO's payment model prior to contracting with that ACO to ensure that the quality of patient care is not threatened by inadequate rates of compensation.
- Members of an ACO should advocate that shared savings payments be calculated primarily on the basis of relevant medical factors, available outcomes data, the costs associated with involved providers, and consensus-oriented standards of necessary care.
- Members should seek agreements with plans that provide sufficient financial resources for all care that is the physician's obligations to deliver and should refuse to sign agreements that fail in this regard.

Notes

1. American Medical Association Opinion 6.12. Forgiveness or Waiver of Insurance Copayments, http://www.ama-assn.org//ama/pub/physician-resources/medical-ethics/code-medical-ethics/opionion512.page.

2. 76 Fed. Reg. 67,801.

3. Matthew DeCamp, *Ethics in Accountable Care Organizations*, AM. MED. ASS'N (Feb. 2013), http://virtualmentor.ama-assn.org/2013/02/pfor1-1302.html.

4. *Id.*

5. http://www.gpo.gov/fdsys/pkg/FR-2011-11-02/pdf/2011-27461.pdf.

6. AM. MED. ASS'N, http://www.ama-assn.org/resources/doc/washington/aco-principles.pdf (last visited Mar. 18, 2014).

7. http://www.gpo.gov/fdsys/pkg/FR-2011–11–02/pdf/2011–27461.pdf.

8. *Id.*

9. DeCamp, *supra* note 2.

10. AM. MED. ASS'N, http://www.ama-assn.org//ama/pub/physician-resources/medical-ethics/code-medical-ethics/opinion304.page (last visited Mar. 18, 2014).

11 Congratulations, You Are an Accountable Care Organization. Now What?

It has been said that the task of getting two physicians to agree with each other is challenging, but the task of getting multiple physicians in multiple groups to agree with each other is potentially overwhelming. In this author's experience, the task of designing and organizing the corporate structure and filling out the Medicare Shared Savings Program (SSP) application pales in comparison to the countless hours of hand-holding and reassurance required to get physicians comfortable enough to move forward to participate in an Accountable Care Organization (ACO). Furthermore, once one gets recognized by the Centers of Medicare and Medicaid Services (CMS) as an ACO, the task of educating providers as to best practices and then keeping each and every practice group stable enough to proceed cohesively also adds to the enormity of the task ahead.

Indeed, there is great reliance upon information technology (IT) infrastructure, and it is advisable to have an ACO IT infrastructure funded/supported by an equity partner, an insurance company, and/or a large health care system that can help shoulder the costs associated with data and outcomes aggregation. In this author's experience, approximately \$1.5 million of capital (in cash or in kind) is required to accomplish the data and IT requirements sufficient to satisfy the CMS guidelines.

"Accountable care" has arrived—both as a way of doing business and an approach to providing "high quality" health care. It is currently the perception of many health care consumers that doctors seem to be compensated more for quantity rather than quality, and some surmise that doctors seem to be ordering more tests to manage legal risk more than to manage the patient medically. With accountable care, the potential for reducing overall health care costs, realigning incentives, and focusing clinical resources on prevention and disease management provides a real opportunity for health care reform.

Medicare providers who participate in an ACO in the SSP will continue to receive payment under Medicare fee-for-service rules. That is, Medicare will continue to pay individual providers and suppliers for specific items and services as it currently does under the Medicare fee-for-service payment systems. However, CMS will also develop a benchmark for each ACO against which ACO performance is measured to assess whether it qualifies to receive shared savings or, for ACOs that have elected to accept responsibility for losses, potentially be held accountable for losses.

The benchmark is an estimate of what the total Medicare fee-for-service Parts A and B expenditures for ACO beneficiaries would otherwise have been in the absence of the ACO, even if all of those services were not provided by providers in the ACO. The benchmark will take into account beneficiary characteristics and other factors that may affect the need for health care services. This benchmark will be updated for each performance year within the agreement period.

The ACO quality measures align with those used in other CMS quality programs, such as the Physician Quality Reporting System and the Electronic Health Record Incentive Programs. The ACO quality measures also align with the National Quality Strategy and other Department of Health and Human Services priorities, such as the Million Hearts Initiative. In developing the final rule, CMS listened to industry concerns about focusing more on outcomes and considered a broad array of measures that would help to assess an ACO's success in delivering high-quality health care at both the individual and population levels. CMS also sought to address comments that supported adopting fewer total measures that reflect processes and outcomes, and aligning the measures with those used in other quality reporting programs, such as the Physician Quality Reporting System.

CMS is encouraging providers to participate in the SSP by setting the quality performance standard to complete and accurate reporting only for the first performance year of the ACO's agreement period and providing a longer phase-in to performance over the second and third performance years. For the first performance year, then, CMS is defining the quality performance standard at the level of complete and accurate reporting for all quality measures.

This means that ACOs will be eligible for the maximum sharing rate (60 percent for the two-sided model and 50 percent for the one-sided model) if the ACO generates sufficient savings and successfully reports the required quality measures. During subsequent performance years, the quality performance standard will be phased in such that ACOs must continue to report all measures but will eventually be assessed on performance. That is, after the first year, the ACO must not only report but also perform well on *selected* quality measures. This flexibility will allow newly formed ACOs a grace period as they start up their operations and learn to work together to better coordinate patient care and improve quality.

Pay-for-performance programs (PFP) will be phased in over the ACO's first agreement period as follows:

- Year 1: Pay-for reporting applies to all 33 measures.
- Year 2: Pay-for-performance applies to 25 measures. Pay-for reporting applies to eight measures.
- Year 3: Pay-for-performance applies to 32 measures. Pay-for reporting applies to one measure that is a survey measure of functional status. CMS will keep the measure in pay for reporting status for the entire agreement period. This will allow ACOs to gain experience with the measure and will provide important information to them on improving the outcomes of their patient populations.

For PFP measures, the minimum attainment level will be set at a national 30 percent or the national 30th percentile of the performance benchmark. Performance benchmarks will be national and established using national fee-for-service claims data, national Medicare Advantage (MA) quality reporting rates, or a flat national percentage for measures where MA or fee-for-service claims data is not available. Performance equal to or greater than the minimum attainment level for a measure will receive points on a sliding scale based on the level of performance. Performance at or above 90 percent or the 90th percentile of the performance benchmark will earn the maximum points available for the measure.

Two of the disease topics under the "at-risk population" domain contain composite measurements. The all-or-nothing scoring means that diabetes and coronary artery disease composite measures will each receive the maximum available points if all criteria of the composite measure are met and zero points if one or more of the criteria are not met. Moreover, six of the Consumer Assessment of Healthcare Providers and Systems (CAHPS) measures are scored together as one measure and one of the CAHPS measures is treated separately. Finally, the Electronic Health Record Incentive Programs participation measure will be double-weighted in order to encourage electronic health record adoption.

CMS will add the points earned for the individual measures within each domain and divide by the total points available for the domain to determine each of the four domain scores. The domains will be weighted equally and scores averaged to determine the ACO's overall quality performance score and sharing rate. ACOs would need to achieve the minimum attainment level on at least 70 percent of the measures in each domain to avoid being placed on a corrective action plan. In addition to the measures used for the quality performance standards for shared savings eligibility, CMS will also use certain measures for monitoring purposes to ensure ACOs are not avoiding at-risk patients or engaging in overuse, underuse, or misuse of health care services.

A major part of the ACO design is that health care providers are more involved managing the health and care of a population with some level of attendant risk for the amount of care provided. ACOs do require significant provider involvement, but multiple groups can provide the direction or leadership in the creation of the ACO. Specific entities that sponsor the ACO come in many types, but four general categories have emerged: (1) hospital systems, (2) physician groups, (3) insurers, and (4) community-based organizations. Community-based organizations are nonprofit, nonmedical entities that bring together the payers and providers that will contract to form the actual ACO.

A year after the passage of the Affordable Care Act (first quarter 2011), hospital-system-led ACOs outnumbered all other types at a rate of 2-to-1, but there were still relatively few (71) ACOs. By the end of 2011, ACOs had doubled in number; hospitals still accounted for a majority of all ACOs, but physician groups and insurers saw faster relative growth. In 2012 and the beginning of 2013, ACOs have nearly tripled in number again, with growth coming among all types of sponsoring entities. Of the 282 new ACOs in this period, 158 (56 percent) are sponsored by physician groups, 103 (36.5 percent) by hospital systems, 17 (6 percent) by insurers, and 4 (1.5 percent) by community-based organizations. The initial movement of ACOs was led by hospital systems, but physician groups have now surpassed them as the most common sponsoring entity among all ACOs. Health insurers, though they may not appear as the sponsoring entity, continue to play a strong role in ACO formation with financial backing and a willingness to explore novel payment models. At the time of this writing, there are an estimated 500 ACOs in the United States.

While physician group-led ACOs are most numerous, they are generally smaller than those run by hospitals. CMS reports that approximately half of all Medicare ACOs are physician-led organizations that serve fewer than 10,000 beneficiaries, meaning hospital-led ACOs in the SSP must have, on average, at least twice as many patients as those led by physician groups to cover the estimated 4 million Medicare beneficiaries. The authors' research has found similar results among private sector ACOs, with hospital-led ACOs having, on average, considerably larger ACO populations than those led by physician groups. While physician groups now sponsor the majority of ACOs, hospital systems still oversee the larger volume of total ACO patients.

Currently, there are some significant differences across ACO models in how they try to achieve savings and manage their patient population—particularly between those sponsored by hospital systems and physician groups. Physician groups have the general approach that ACOs save money by keeping a patient out of the hospital and seek to accomplish this by managing patient care in outpatient settings, such as by using patient-centered medical homes to coordinate care among specialists. Hospital-system-led ACOs, meanwhile, focus on better managing patients once they have been admitted to a hospital by trying to coordinate care among departments and providers. Both types of entities are trying to break down artificial silos so that the appropriate providers will work together to treat the patient at the proper time, as well as follow best practices and more effectively monitor their patient population.

Each of these approaches has merit, but the ideal ACO will focus on keeping patients from entering a hospital and cost-effectively treating those that are admitted. A major challenge to achieving this lies in sharing governance for the ACO and responsibility for a patient population between organizations that are capable of efficiently managing patient care across the whole continuum of health care services. Within a level of health care providers, great strides are being made to improve care coordination, but between care levels (such as between inpatient and outpatient), there is less progress being made.

If a large physician group or a hospital system can achieve savings by working alone, they have little incentive to partner with another provider group as equals to further improve patient care. The next step in the accountable care movement will require a recognition that levels and locations of care are artificial constructs and that patient care should instead be focused on treating the patient appropriately; whether the care is being reimbursed by Medicare Part A, B, or D or a private payer should matter much less than focusing on connecting patients with the right provider in the right location for their illness acuity. This, though, will require large physician groups and hospital systems (and eventually post-acute-care and long-term-care providers) to work together and align their goals around patient care. This does not require wholesale integration of providers, but that may be the result in some markets.

The accountable care movement is progressing rapidly as many provider groups throughout the nation are officially adopting the title of ACO and are adopting some form of contract that encourages population management and cost minimization. While ACO growth will undoubtedly continue for at least the immediate future, it still represents a small minority of care delivered in the United States. Whether the numerous organizations that are cautiously observing ACOs from the side will ever take the plunge and adopt accountable care models will largely depend on the success of these early adopters. It is certainly much easier to adopt a new payment model when peer institutions achieve success rather than end up millions in the hole.

From the authors perspective, ACOs are still a work in progress, and their eventual success or failure is still to be determined. In 2013, many ACOs will complete their first year under a risk-based ACO contract, and their early results will influence how payers, providers, and policymakers experiment with future iterations of accountable care. If the results are good, then the ACO model may become the dominant form of health care in the United States over the next decade. If the results are negative, accountable care may never gain a permanent foothold in our delivery system. The health care system will be watching to see how the accountable care movement plays out.

Health care providers who are not ready or prepared to transition their practices to operate in a manner required under accountable care models will ever-increasingly find themselves in an uncompetitive position. They will find their patients gravitating toward physicians that are taking a more coordinated approach to health care due to benefit design changes in private health plans, governmental programs, and hospital-physician clinical integration activities. Moreover, governmental and third-party payers will also favor ACOs, as they have "mastered" patient outcomes and reporting strategies in order to deliver more efficient and cost-effective health care.

On the other hand, this author also believes that as we hit the "brick wall" glut of baby boomers in the United States demanding health care, the free market will also play a major role in meeting the needs of consumers in this country. In fact, what will probably emerge are three tiers of health care to handle patient populations: (1) government-sponsored and commercial insurance health care through insurance exchanges, (2) charity care from private nonprofit organizations, and (3) cash-only consumers receiving medical care from boutique health care providers and facilities.

Some physicians perceive ACOs as a threat to their economic viability and as a means for the government to take their money out of the system and put more control—somebody else's control—into the system. There is some truth to that perception, but an effective ACO model theoretically embraces physician and patient decision making, and uses physician expertise to design a more patient-oriented care delivery model. This new model can then be achieved with technology, business model process redesigns, and aligned incentives so that care is done in the most effective and efficient manner. Done right, this approach will conceivably deliver greater value for everyone involved, including the physician.

As our health care-hungry populations grow, the United States will be forced to practice population medicine: Some patients in the population will slip through the cracks, some will die, but statistically most of the population will receive some type of health care. Using innovation and technology effectively and creatively will provide answers to the delivery of efficient health care—but it is incumbent upon the health care providers or those that would organize and manage these providers into entities that provide health care for future generations.

For many physicians, some of the key questions in their mind are: How will I get paid in the future? How should the health care delivery model synchronize with the payment models? What changes must my staff embrace for the new model to work? Do I have the right people? What is the patient's experience? What must I do individually and what must we do as a group to get there?

The enforcement of the Affordable Care Act (ACA) provides physicians with the opportunity to come together with like-minded professionals and create a health care system that capitalizes on the physicians' skills as a health care provider for the benefit of his or her patients. Forming an ACO is not easy, and it is critically important for physicians considering an ACO to take the time to meet all the "partners" they will have in that ACO to make sure they will be comfortable referring their patients to those other health care providers within that ACO.

Although the ACA does not *require* physicians to refer only within their ACO—it stands to reason that in order to keep the outcomes data "within the family," it will also be important to keep the referrals within the ACO so that there is no "leakage" out of one's ACO into a competing ACO. The authors would like to emphasize the importance of establishing an IT infrastructure that goes way beyond the traditional electronic medical record. The health care provider of the future must be able to utilize technology that provides much greater access to patient information, clinical guidance, and business intelligence to track and manage patient care outcomes. Unfortunately, the traditional electronic medical records—even when integrated to Health Information Exchanges—are an inadequate foundation for accountable care. Having a clear understanding of how technology can make an ACO successful is critical to success in the post-reform health care industry.

Some authors believe that the compensation models afforded by ACOs can actually give physicians more control over the care model they want to create—spending more time than they currently spend addressing patients' health care needs before they become ill. The emphasis on preventive care and patient outreach should lead to more satisfied patients over time while at the same time providing greater financial gains to those physicians whose care models result in better overall patient care. Others, however, believe that the exercise is futile because the true "accountability" should rest equally with the patient, rather than the physician.

Therein lies the rub: If the health care provider is made accountable through regulation, but there is no regulation keeping the patient accountable, how is the health care ecosystem to survive? In the United States, as much as 80 percent of our health care dollars are spent on five diseases (hypertension, diabetes, vascular disease, chronic obstructive pulmonary disease, and morbid obesity)—all of which are preventable. If the entire burden of health care is placed upon health care providers to manage chronic diseases that may be prevented if patients were only held accountable, does that really create a sustainable model for health care?

If anything, this author believes that the ACA will only create a greater division between the different tiers of health care, and until patients are held accountable for their health care—even if it is in the form of regulation or taxation—the "ground rules" for the SSP will likely not be sustainable. Nevertheless, this is the current law of the land, and it is critically important for those involved in health care at any level to be familiar with the legal developments that evolve in these interesting times.

Index